RUNNER'S WORLD®
HOW TO MAKE
YOURSELF POOP

RUNNER'S WORLD®

HOW TO MAKE YOURSELF POOP

AND 999 OTHER TIPS ALL RUNNERS SHOULD KNOW

MEGHAN KITA

RODALE.

Copyright © 2018 by Hearst Magazines, Inc.
Illustrations copyright © by Charlie Layton

All rights reserved.
Published in the United States by Rodale Books, an imprint of the Crown Publishing Group, a division of Penguin Random House LLC, New York.
crownpublishing.com
rodalebooks.com

RODALE and the Plant colophon are registered trademarks of Penguin Random House LLC.

RUNNER'S WORLD is a registered trademark of Hearst Magazines, Inc.

Library of Congress Cataloging-in-Publication Data is available.

ISBN 978-1-63565-183-6
Ebook ISBN 978-1-63565-184-3

Printed in the United States of America

Book design by Jordan Wannamaker
Cover design by Charlie Layton

10 9 8 7 6 5 4 3 2

First Edition

For my mom, who helped me hone my sense of humor,

and for Paul, who makes me laugh every day

CONTENTS

SECTION 5:
169 TIPS FOR STAYING HEALTHY 151

SECTION 6: 157 RACING TIPS 193

INTRODUCTION

Welcome to *Runner's World How to Make Yourself Poop and 999 Other Tips All Runners Should Know*. If you bought this book as a gag gift ("hee, hee—poop!"), do we have a surprise for you: The following pages are actually packed full of interesting information—for people who run, people who aspire to run, and people who aren't super into running but give some number of shits about being healthy, fit, and active.

Read on, and you'll learn which songs are best suited for exercise, which snacks will best satisfy your postdinner cravings, how to sleep better in high-stress situations—things that athletes and nonathletes alike can appreciate. We're not going to lie, though: There's plenty of stuff in here that'll mostly appeal to runners. (That's what happens in a *Runner's World*–branded book.)

So whether this book will occupy a place of honor on your shelves, next to classics by running greats like Jeff Galloway and Hal Higdon, or whether it's destined to rest atop your toilet tank—where, let's be honest, more people will probably read it—you'll find something you can use to become healthier, happier, and more regular.

SECTION 1:

205 TRAINING TIPS

THE 5 GOLDEN RULES OF TRAINING

---

1. **THE VAST MAJORITY OF YOUR MILES SHOULD FEEL EASY.** At least 70 percent of your weekly mileage should be run at a comfortable pace.[1] (Easy miles make up 80 percent of the total volume of most professional runners, but they're logging far more than most of us.)[2]

2. **YOUR "EASY EFFORT" SHOULD BE REALLY, REALLY EASY.** Like, supereasy. Like, can talk in complete sentences easy—if you're running solo, you should be able to inhale for three steps and exhale for three steps. Working too hard on easy days is among the most common mistakes coaches see runners make, and it can hinder recovery and even lead to injury.[3]

3. **INCREASE MILEAGE GRADUALLY.** The "10 percent rule" is a good starting point: Bump up your volume by no more than 10 percent each week to stay healthy. If you're coming back from a brief layoff, however, and starting from a single-digit

mileage week, you can increase more rapidly until you're close to your normal amount.[4]

4. **AIM FOR THREE.** To run your best, include three quality workouts each week: a speed workout, a long run, and an in-between workout at a comfortably hard pace (a "tempo run").[5] Your speedwork should include hard bursts (at 5K pace or slightly faster) that last from 30 seconds to a mile, with walking or jogging recovery periods interspersed.[6] Your long run should be done at an easy effort and should be long enough to comprise 20 to 30 percent of your weekly mileage.[7] Begin your tempo runs with at least 10 minutes of jogging to warm up, then spend at least 20 minutes pushing the pace before cooling down.[8]

5. **FOLLOW EVERY HARD OR LONG RUN WITH AT LEAST ONE EASY OR REST DAY.** Less experienced and older runners may need up to 3 days between tough efforts. (You'll only fit in two key workouts per week, but as long as you're doing speedwork, tempo runs, and long efforts regularly, you'll still perform well.)[9] Listen to your body: If your legs don't feel fresh early in a speed session or long run, schedule another in-between day next week.

ONE

PLANNING YOUR TRAINING

5 RUNNING FREQUENCIES (AND HOW TO TELL WHICH IS RIGHT FOR YOU)[1]

Choosing how many days per week to run is like finding a life partner: You just know when it's right. But unlike your partner (hopefully), your perfect frequency might change as you age and evolve as an athlete. Here's how to know how many run days are right for you, right now.

1. **ONE OR TWO RUNNING DAYS PER WEEK.** If you're coming back from illness or injury—or your life has gone completely bonkers—something always beats nothing. If you can add in walks or cross-training to boost fitness without much impact, that will prepare your body to run more when the time is right.

2. **THREE RUNNING DAYS.** This is an ideal frequency for triathletes, low-mileage runners, or the injury-prone. You'll want each run to last at least 20 minutes. If you have dreams of fast finishes but always end up hurt, you may be able to reach your goals with 1 speedwork day, 1 tempo-run day, and 1 long-run day, plus 2 days of cross-training; pick up the book *Run Less, Run Faster* for plans.

3. **FOUR OR FIVE RUNNING DAYS.** Most longtime runners settle in here, the "sweet spot" for those who log miles as their primary exercise and aren't frequently injured. These runners can safely manage 30 to 50 weekly miles with ample time to recover. Most half- and full-marathon plans will have you running 4 or 5 days.

4. **SIX RUNNING DAYS.** More advanced runners might land here, especially when training for a half- or full-marathon PR. The more often you run, the better you'll be—if your body and schedule will allow it.

5. **SEVEN RUNNING DAYS.** This is the realm of streakers, elite runners, and obsessives. If you're young and healthy, you might be able to handle this frequency. Just make sure to run at a truly easy pace the days before and after hard or long workouts.

4 REASONS TO RUN WITHOUT RACING[2]

If anyone tells you you're not a real runner because you don't race, sock 'em right in the nose. Running makes you a runner—and it's easier to stick to a running routine if you know why you're doing it. If you're not running to race, find what else motivates you to determine how you should train.

1. **TO BE HEALTHY AND FIT.** You'll want to run about every other day and no more than about 35 miles per week to get the most benefits from running with the least risk of injury. Round out your week with an additional day or two of cross-training or strength training that challenges your body in a different way. Choose a few activities that you enjoy and switch it up if you get bored.

2. **TO LOSE WEIGHT.** In addition to a couple easy runs, schedule one long run (of 45 to 90 minutes) and one high-intensity interval session each week. Try Chicago-based coach Jenny

Hadfield's "fat-blaster workout": Walk and jog 6 minutes to warm up, then do eight to ten 60-second all-out bursts with 90-second walking recoveries. Light to moderate strength training promotes a leaner physique, so find a way to work it into your routine at least twice per week.

3. **TO RELIEVE STRESS.** High-intensity efforts can *create* stress, so stick to an easy pace most days. If you know you feel better postrun, try easy doubles (two 20- to 30-minute runs, one in the morning and one in the afternoon or evening) instead of a single longer outing. Research shows your mood improves when you're outdoors, so when possible, avoid the treadmill.

4. **TO BE SOCIAL.** Joining up with a group for a long, easy run is a sure way to make running buddies. If that seems too intimidating, offer to join a wannabe runner on his or her first outings—it's fun to be a role model. Or enjoy some pre- and postrun interaction without the pressure to chat as you run by joining a group track or hill workout.

---

2 REASONS TO TRAIN BY TIME . . . [3]

Research shows that your brain processes time and distance differently. When you're going for time, you're more likely to maintain an even effort; when you're going for distance, you're more likely to pick it up as you near the end. Both methods have a place in your training—here is time's.

1. **TO LEARN HOW TO GAUGE EFFORT.** Time-based intervals and tempo runs require you to home in on an effort you can sustain for the duration of the repeat—a skill you need if you race. You'll tune in to your breathing and body to replicate the feeling you experience hitting what you've learned to be your speedwork or tempo pace in distance-based workouts.

2. **TO GIVE YOUR BRAIN A BREAK.** If it's really warm or windy, or you're coming back from illness or injury, you'll struggle to

hit your perfect-day paces during workouts—and that might sap your confidence. Instead, translate your usual workout to a time- and effort-based one. For example, if you usually run 800-meter repeats in 4:00 each with 400-meter recovery, do 4:00 hard repeats with 2:00 jogging recovery off the track. Or if your long-run pace is 10:00 per mile and you have 12 on the schedule on a warm, humid day, run at a comfortable pace for 2 hours. Easy-run days are also good to do by time instead of distance: Run slowly enough to avoid huffing and puffing for 30 to 60 minutes.

. . . AND 2 TO TRAIN BY DISTANCE[4]

1. **TO SET A GOAL PACE.** If you never know how fast you're running, you won't know how fast you can expect to finish on race day. Some runners are cool with this, but if you're not, you'll need to go for distance in at least some of your workouts. Measure key workouts at least every 2 to 3 weeks to see how you're progressing.
2. **TO LEARN A GOAL PACE.** If you have a pace in mind, the best way to ensure you can do it on race day is to practice it. You can use speedwork repeats of up to a mile to rehearse 5K or 10K pace. Half and full marathoners can dedicate a mid-length weekday run to practicing pace; more experienced athletes can build race-pace miles into their long runs every other week instead.

2 RULES TO HELP YOU INCREASE MILEAGE SAFELY[5]

Running too much is a recipe for disaster—or at least for shin splints. But it's possible to gradually raise the threshold of what your body considers "too much." Either follow a reputable training plan to boost mileage slowly and safely or follow one of these rules.

1. **THE 10 PERCENT RULE.** This oft-repeated nugget recommends increasing volume by no more than 10 percent each week. For example, if you're running 20 miles this week, run no more than 22 next week.

2. **THE ACUTE-TO-CHRONIC TRAINING RATIO.** This more-scientific rule compares your "acute" mileage from the previous week to your "chronic" mileage (the average of your 4 previous weeks). For example, if you ran 20 miles in week 1, 22 in week 2, 24 in week 3, and 28 in week 4, that gives you an average mileage of 23.5. Divide your "acute" mileage (28, in week 4) by your average (23.5) to get the ratio (1.19). Research has found that injury risk increases when the ratio is 1.2 or higher and increases significantly when it's more than 1.5. This rule is useful for upping mileage *and* for plotting a safe return from illness or injury.

THE 4-STEP PLAN FOR IMPROVING AS A RUNNER—WITHOUT GETTING HURT[6]

The Road Runners Club of America (RRCA) offers a 2-day coaching certification program that thousands of runners have completed. In it, students learn about "Introduce, Improve, Perfect" (IIP), a term for 3-week training cycles that originates with coaches Randy Accetta, PhD, and Greg Wenneborg. If you want to plan your own training, this principle will help you progress safely. Learn it and love it.

1. **INTRODUCE.** In the first of the 3 weeks, you'll add one new workout while keeping the rest of your week the same. For example, if you've been logging 25 easy miles per week, you might turn an easy weekday 5-miler into an interval run that adds up to the same mileage—4 x 800 meters at 10K pace with 400-meter recovery, plus a mile of warmup and cooldown, for example—and leave the rest of your week alone.

2. **IMPROVE.** In the second week, you'll alter the key workout to

be a little bit more difficult—by adding a repetition, shortening the recovery, or speeding up the pace—without changing the rest of your runs.

3. **PERFECT.** In the third week, you'll increase the difficulty of the key workout once more. If you added a rep in week 2, add one more. If you sped up to between 5K and 10K pace in week 2, try to hit 5K pace in week 3. If you cut recovery time from 400 meters to 300 in week 2, cut it to 200 in week 3.

4. **REPEAT.** After this 3-week cycle, choose another workout to IIP. You may start lengthening your long or tempo runs or add in hill work that gets progressively harder.

4 WAYS TO RUN FARTHER AND FASTER WITH LESS EFFORT[7]

That almost sounds like a snake-oil-salesman promise. But if you train to improve your running economy, you'll boost your endurance *and* speed, all in one fell swoop. Try these tactics and you'll see that it's not too good to be true.

1. **LOG MORE MILES.** It's simple: The more you run, the better your body becomes at running—even if those miles feel easy. Add 5 minutes to each outing or change one rest day to an easy 30-minute run to get started.

2. **ADD SOME SPEED.** If you're not already doing speedwork, start. As you tax your body, it finds ways to do what you're demanding with less effort. Start with eight to ten 30-second pickups during one run per week, and once you're comfortable with that, switch to weekly interval training at 5K to 10K pace.

3. **STRENGTH TRAIN STRATEGICALLY.** Research shows that intense strength training improves running economy. "Intense" means lifting to failure: doing moves like squats, lunges, and deadlifts with enough weight or reps that you can't do another. You may be sore afterward, so do this later in the

same day as a hard or long run, and rest or run easy the following 2 days.

4. **HIT THE HILLS.** You recruit more muscle fibers while climbing than you do while running on flat terrain, so even working hills into your easy runs will help. For a more intense hill workout, try repeats: On a moderate slope, do six to eight 45- to 60-second pickups, starting at 5K effort and progressing to all-out. Recover completely—with 90 seconds of jogging and walking—between reps.

10 SAFETY RULES EVERY RUNNER SHOULD KNOW[8]

Unless you're a treadmill-only runner, logging miles requires going out into the unpredictable and potentially dangerous world. Luckily, you're not helpless: There's plenty you can do to maximize your chances of an uneventful run—or to stay as safe as possible in the unlikely event of a problem.

1. **SHARE YOUR PLANS.** Before heading out, tell a family member or friend the route you're planning to run and about when you should be back.

2. **CARRY ID.** Another "just in case" measure is to make sure helpers can identify you (and phone your emergency contact) if you're not able to respond midrun.

3. **CHANGE IT UP.** Varying your routes and the time of day that you run makes it harder for strangers to know where you'll be and when.

4. **BE VISIBLE . . .** If any part of your run will take place in low light, wear brightly colored, reflective clothing and carry lights: Ones that blink or move (like handheld lights or those you attach to your shoes) are easiest for drivers to spot.[9]

5. **. . . BUT ASSUME YOU'RE NOT.** Unless a driver makes eye contact with you and waves you across the road, act as if he or

she didn't see you. Don't expect every driver to stop, signal, or otherwise follow the rules of the road.

6. **RUN FACING TRAFFIC (USUALLY).** It's easier for drivers to see you (and for you to see them) if you're on the left side of the road. Exceptions include when you're approaching blind curves or working your way up a steep hill: Run with traffic temporarily whenever a road obstructs your view of oncoming traffic.

7. **BEWARE DISTRACTIONS.** If you must run with headphones, keep the volume low and one ear completely clear. Loud music drowns out approaching vehicles, barking dogs, and other potential threats, and headphones make you appear to be an easy target to any dangerous people you might encounter.[10]

8. **KEEP YOUR COOL.** In most cases, responding to an angry driver or catcaller will only escalate the situation. When possible, ignore and move on. But if you feel threatened, head to a safe, public place and call for help.

9. **PREPARE FOR ANIMALS.** If you do most of your running in neighborhoods or parks, dogs are likely the most intimidating "wildlife" you'll see. If one is off-leash and takes interest in you, slow to a walk or stop, remain upright and calm, and use a

firm voice to say "stop," "sit," or "no."[11] If you run on trails or rural roads, learn how to identify and respond to regional threats such as bears, snakes, and the like.

10. **WHEN IN DOUBT, BRING A FRIEND (OR A FEW).** You've known since you were little that there's safety in numbers, and it holds true when you run. It's easier for drivers to spot pairs or groups, and run squads are less attractive than individuals to people seeking to do harm.

WHY YOU SHOULD TRAIN ON THESE 3 TYPES OF TERRAIN[12]

It's convenient to just head out your door for runs in your neighborhood, but if that means you're always on flat ground (or intense hills, or the rolling terrain in between), it's time to suck it up and explore some new routes. Changing up your go-tos can fix imbalances that lead to injury. Plus, you'll kick major ass no matter what the elevation profile of your goal race looks like. Work each of these terrain types into your training.

1. **HILLY.** We're talking about routes with a climb (or a few) that's long and/or steep enough that you dread it. Conquering this type of hill builds strength and cardiovascular clout in a way that's similar to speedwork without the impact forces. (And you might even enjoy a view from the top!) Hit big hills once or twice every 2 weeks.

2. **FLAT.** The repetitive motion of running on superflat terrain can spell trouble on race day if you haven't trained for it. Level ground is also best for going your fastest or practicing perfect pacing. Choose it for most speed or tempo workouts; do a few on race-like terrain if your goal event has hills. To prep for a flat half or full marathon, do at least half of your long runs on pancake-like routes.

3. **ROLLING.** This is the happy medium for day-to-day runs: not hard enough to *really* work your legs and lungs, but not flat

enough to cause repetitive-motion injury. When possible, do most of your runs in this in-between space. If you're a flat-lander, add bridges (or a handful of short, easy-effort stair-climbs) to the middle of easy runs to mix up the stress on your legs.

7 TRAIL-RUNNING TIPS FOR ROAD RUNNERS[13]

Going off-road can be both exciting (there are no cars!) and scary (there are wild animals!). To make your first trail experiences as pleasant and medical-emergency-free as possible, follow these rules.

1. **CHOOSE WISELY.** If you only run on asphalt, start on a fairly level gravel, dirt, or wood-chip trail to adjust to the softer surface. If you're already accustomed to softness, pick a trail without overly technical terrain—anything super rocky, rooty, or otherwise easy to trip on.

2. **BRING A FRIEND.** It's smart to trail-run with others for safety reasons. When you're a noob, find someone you trust to show you around a route that's appropriate for your ability, and at an equally appropriate pace.

3. **AVOID WIPING OUT.** If you're behind another runner, maintain a safe following distance. You need to be able to scan the ground a few meters in front of you to anticipate obstacles. Slowing way down also helps prevent falls.

4. **RUN FOR TIME.** It'll take you longer to cover your usual distances on trails—especially hilly ones—so stay out there only as long as you would on a typical easy-run day.

5. **BE PREPARED.** Know that stabilizing muscles in your feet, ankles, and shins may be sore for a couple days postrun—they don't have to work nearly as hard to keep you upright on roads.

6. **STAY ALERT.** Headphones and trails don't mix. You need to be able to hear people who want to pass, since many trails aren't

wide enough to accommodate more than one runner or cyclist across.

7. **KNOW THE LOCAL FLORA AND FAUNA.** If you live in bear, snake, or mountain lion country, learn how to protect yourself *before* you head anywhere you might encounter such creatures. Same goes for dangerous plants—a big patch of poison ivy is a bad place to make an emergency pit stop.

HOW TO PLAN YOUR TRAINING AROUND 4 BUSY-PERSON SITUATIONS[14]

If you *always* find time to complete every single workout, you probably could stand to reduce your caffeine intake. Most of us have to let a ball drop from time to time, and that's okay. Here are some workarounds for when life strikes.

1. **YOU WERE UP ALL NIGHT TENDING TO A BIG PROJECT OR SICK KID.** One night of bad sleep shouldn't hurt your performance too much, so proceed as planned. A few nights of bad sleep, though, and you'll benefit more from sleeping in than from slogging through your run.

2. **YOU HAVE TO MISS A WORKOUT . . .** This is fine, once in a while. If it happens every week, you'll need to find a training plan more compatible with your situation—even if that means a slower finishing time.

3. **. . . OR TWO WORKOUTS . . .** Prioritize the one that's most aligned with your goals. If you're training for a half or full marathon, your long run trumps all other runs. Those who are looking to race short and fast, or lose weight, should be sure to complete their speedwork.

4. **. . . OR YOU'VE LOST COUNT BECAUSE YOU'RE ALWAYS TIME-CRUNCHED.** 'Tis the season to do what you can, when you can. If two 30-minute sessions fit your schedule better than a single, hour-long one, double up. If your kid wakes up

halfway through a treadmill interval session, cut it short and resume it later if you can. Do your best and don't lose your mind.

8 STRATEGIES FOR NOT TOTALLY LETTING YOURSELF GO WHILE YOU'RE ON VACATION[15]

First of all, if you want to let yourself go on vacation, do it: A week or two of sloth and gluttony isn't going to ruin your fitness forever. Those who want to say yes to both running *and* vacation indulgences should try this.

1. **DO SOMETHING BIG BEFORE YOU LEAVE.** A day or two before vacation begins, do a hard workout or long run. That way, you can rest or run easy on your travel day and your first day in town.

2. **SHOOT FOR MAINTENANCE . . .** You'll stay running-fit if you manage to cover at least 40 percent of your usual weekly mileage while on vacation.[16]

3. **. . . BUT REMEMBER THAT SOMETHING BEATS NOTHING.** Even if you can't find a window for a run most days, you can squeeze in some squats and burpees in your room, or you can alternate between reading on the beach and taking a brisk walk along the surf. Whatever you can do to engage your muscles and raise your heart rate helps.

4. **GO FIRST THING.** Your best shot at squeezing in a run is before everyone else is dressed and ready to eat breakfast. (It's coolest then, too.)

5. **USE RUNS TO EXPLORE.** Ask the concierge or Airbnb host to recommend interesting or scenic areas within a few miles of where you're staying. (Remember to also ask if the route there and back is safe for pedestrians.) Then, do a run-by: You may find shops, restaurants, or other attractions you can return to with your companions later.

6. **BE A TOURIST.** Even if you rarely carry your smartphone,

now's the time to do it. Selfie breaks are encouraged when you're somewhere noteworthy.

7. **FIND LOCAL RUNNERS.** Join up with a specialty store's group run or enter a 5K or 10K race. When you chat with folks who live nearby, you get the best running *and* nonrunning recommendations.

8. **TRY OTHER THINGS.** Hiking, biking, and hours of sightseeing on foot all burn calories and tax your muscles in a way running doesn't.

TWO

GETTING READY TO RUN

---

6 STRATEGIES FOR BECOMING
A MORNING RUNNER

It doesn't matter what time of day you run, but many people find that they're least likely to get sidetracked by other responsibilities if they head out first thing. The trouble is, a body at rest wants to stay at rest—especially if said body is accustomed to sleeping in. Try these steps to develop a new routine.

1. **PLAN TO MEET A FRIEND WHO'S ALREADY A MORNING RUNNER.** This is a make-or-break measure—you'll be far more likely to get out the door if you know someone will be mad if you don't show. Once you've developed the habit, you can fly solo, but enlist help for the first few weeks.

2. **PREP THE NIGHT BEFORE.** Think about your usual prerun routine and do whatever you can the evening prior so your groggy morning self doesn't have to. Check the weather, lay out your clothes and shoes, set up the coffeemaker, put a banana or other morning snack on the counter, and know exactly where you're going and when. And don't forget to get a good night of

sleep: Hit the hay about 10 minutes earlier than usual, and spend the hour before bedtime away from screens and bright lights.

3. **MAKE A FOOLPROOF WAKE-UP PLAN.** For many people, getting out of bed to shut off the alarm is enough to ensure they're up. For those who can rise, hit snooze, and conk out again, you'll have to get creative. Maybe this means getting an alarm on wheels that you need to chase to turn off. (It doubles as a warmup!) In extreme cases, you can give a spare key to your running buddy, so he or she can barge in and physically remove you from bed.

4. **JOLT YOURSELF AWAKE.** Once you're up, turn on ALL the lights. Light is a powerful signal to your brain that says, "Hello! Good morning! It's time to start the day!"

5. **EXPERIMENT.** What, when, and how much you should eat and drink before an early run is something you have to figure out by trial and error. You're likely at least a little dehydrated in the morning, so have a glass of water. If you'll be gone longer than 60 minutes, you'll probably need to eat something. Try snacks that have agreed with you before afternoon or evening outings. Expect to have some crummy runs before you learn what works for you.

6. **TRY A MANTRA.** When you struggle to get out the door, remember why you're doing this. Whether it's "I like spending evenings with my family" or "running first thing fills me with energy," reminding yourself of why your miles can't wait helps get your rear in gear.

---

3 WAYS TO MAKE YOURSELF POOP[1]

If you've ever had to start a run before your bowels were ready, you know how crucial it is to clear out before heading out. An urgent need to find a bathroom (or a semiprivate clump of bushes) can turn an otherwise pleasant run to crap. Here's how to ensure you do your business before you get down to business.

1. **COFFEE (OR TEA, OR HOT WATER) AND CHILL.** Any warm liquid should work: Studies have found regular and decaf coffee have the same poo-inducing effect. Choose your favorite hot beverage and drink it at least 30 minutes before go time.

2. **WARM UP NEAR A TOILET.** Motion can bring on a BM, as anyone who has needed a potty break just minutes into a run can attest. An added bonus: Warming up prerun enlivens your muscles and gets your heart pumping. Try a dynamic warmup routine before leaving home—with moves like jumping jacks, walking lunges, and skips—or just jog around the block until you're ready to make.

3. **"YOU WANT ME TO MASSAGE WHERE?!?"** If all else fails, you can try putting gentle pressure on your perineum, the area between your genitals and your anus. A 2014 study from UCLA found this may help ease constipation.[2]

THE 3 ELEMENTS OF A PERFECT WARMUP[3]

Okay, okay—there is no single perfect warmup. Newer runners, those who are just coming back from injury, and those who are about to run hard need a more thorough warmup than experienced, healthy runners heading out for some easy miles. The point is to prime your body for activity by increasing blood flow, body temperature, and heart rate so you perform your best and avoid hurting yourself. Here's how.

1. **WALKING AND/OR JOGGING.** Start with at least 3 to 5 minutes of easy movement to transition from couch to road. If you're more experienced, this might just mean walking around the house to collect and put on your running gear. Then run easy for at least 10 to 15 minutes—that's enough of a warmup for a tempo run.

2. **STRIDES.** These, also known as pickups, are a series of gradual accelerations over about 100 meters. Walk for about 60 seconds between each, and do about six total. If you're doing these before speedwork, the last couple should peak around the pace you're targeting for your repeats.

3. **DYNAMIC STRETCHES.** Drills like skips, walking toe touches, walking lunges, and leg swings improve elasticity, reducing your injury risk. The faster you're planning to run— or the more injury-prone you are—the more important it is to warm up in this way.

THREE

MIDRUN TROUBLESHOOTING

3 WAYS TO ERASE A SIDE STITCH WITHOUT STOPPING

Side stitches are likely caused by a cramp in your diaphragm, the muscle beneath your rib cage that helps you breathe.[1] They also hurt like crazy and happen to just about every runner from time to time. Walking it off is an effective strategy, but if you'd rather keep running, these strategies may help.

1. **SLOW DOWN AND BREATHE RHYTHMICALLY.** Time your breathing so you begin each exhalation as the foot on the opposite side of the stitch hits the ground. For example, if the stitch is on your right side, begin exhaling on a left footfall. Try breathing in for two or three steps and then out for the same number of steps. Take deep-belly breaths: Focus on breathing into the area beneath your rib cage and keeping your abs relaxed.[2]

2. **STRETCH YOUR ARMS OVER YOUR HEAD.** Lean slightly to the side opposite the stitch for a bigger stretch.[3]

3. **PRESS ON THE SITE OF THE STITCH.** Put gentle, consistent

pressure on the affected area. Remain upright and continue to take deep breaths as you do so.[4]

---

5 PROBLEMS A SHORT WALK BREAK CAN SOLVE

Some runners view walking midrun as a total-last-resort option that's nearly synonymous with failure. However, there's a reason that Olympian and coach Jeff Galloway, who popularized the run-walk-run strategy,[5] is so well known: Walk breaks can be a useful tool, for beginners and grizzled vets, on everyday runs and during workouts. In some cases, they can make a workout *more* effective. Here are some issues walk breaks can remedy.

1. **HUFFING AND PUFFING.** Walk breaks can help new runners keep their breathing under control, which makes it easier and more enjoyable to run long distances.[6] Experienced runners, however, can still benefit from walk breaks in workouts that involve short, all-out bursts, like hill sprints or repetitions no longer than 200 meters.[7] These workouts are designed to build power and strength, and you'll do so more effectively if your body can recover fully between reps. Try walking for 1 to 2 minutes between all-out reps, or however long it takes to feel nearly 100 percent again.[8]

2. **AN ANGRY STOMACH.** Running inhibits digestion by diverting blood flow away from the digestive system and toward working muscles.[9] A walk break can help reboot your digestive process, which may temper nausea, and it can also help runners who have trouble taking in or processing midrun fuel.[10]

3. **FATIGUED LEG MUSCLES.** Newer runners trying to go farther than ever—or trying to tackle challenging hills—can ease the burden on their legs by taking planned walk breaks.[11] More experienced runners can also benefit, especially during long workouts on unfamiliar terrain. If you usually run rolling

routes, for example, and you find yourself on a long, flat run, your legs might feel zapped from using the same muscles in the same way for so long.[12] A short walk phase gives your flat-terrain running muscles a break.

4. **A SIDE STITCH.** Walking and breathing deeply and rhythmically (exhaling when the foot on the opposite side of the stitch hits the ground) is the most effective way to rid yourself of a stitch.[13]

5. **MENTAL DRAIN.** Whether you're a new or experienced runner, you'll occasionally find yourself in a tough place, mentally. One way to fight that is by taking planned walk breaks from the start of your run.[14] You might use this tactic on every run, or if you're more experienced, during recovery runs the day after a hard or long workout.

THE FEMALE RUNNER'S 2-STEP PLAN FOR DISCREETLY PEEING MIDRUN[15]

Before a run, most men can hydrate and caffeinate with reckless abandon, because male anatomy makes it easy to urinate almost anywhere quickly and discreetly. Female anatomy isn't so accommodating. Plus, the internal pressure generated by a pregnancy can cause urgency,[16] and some women struggle with incontinence after giving birth.[17] To make it easier to relieve yourself when there's no potty (porta- or otherwise) in sight, try this.

1. **DRESS FOR SUCCESS.** In tights or capris, there's no way to wee without dropping trou. Shorts are a better option. The baggier variety with built-in briefs as well as shorter compres-

BONUS TIP If you don't mind toting something, products designed to help people with female anatomy pee outdoors while camping and hiking can also be useful on the run. Do an Internet search for "urinary funnel"—both disposable and reusable models are available.

sion shorts can be shifted aside. The best bet, however, is a running skirt, one with built-in briefs or a briefless option paired with bun-huggers. Briefs can easily be pushed aside beneath the skirt, and the two-piece option allows you to remove the briefs entirely. Black is the smartest color choice because it hides splashes well and matches everything.

2. **TAKE A KNEE.** Once you've found some privacy, lower to your right knee, with your right foot behind you and your left leg bent at a 90-degree angle in front of you. Take the fabric of the right side of your shorts in your hands with one in front of you and one behind you, and shift it toward your left leg. This should create space to let it flow. Kneeling just in front of a tree offers additional protection –passersby might simply think you're lunging.

FOUR

GETTING FASTER

---

7 FUN, SIMPLE FARTLEK (HEE, HEE) WORKOUTS[1]

"Fartlek," which is Swedish for "speed play," is a favorite word among runners for obvious reasons. It refers to unstructured speedwork, like the workouts below. Fast running makes you fitter—and you don't have to obsess over splits and paces to get there. Warm up for 10 minutes, spend 10 to 20 minutes doing the fartlek workout of your choice, and finish with a 5- to 10-minute cooldown.

1. **LANDMARK FARTLEK.** Run hard toward an object up ahead (a mailbox, a parked car, a tree) then slow to a jog once you've passed it. Once you've recovered, choose a new landmark and repeat.
2. **STRAIGHTS AND CURVES.** On a track, push the pace on the straightaways and jog the curves.
3. **GEAR SHIFTER.** Hold your easy pace for a few minutes, shift to tempo effort for 1 minute, then run a hard pace for 30 seconds. Repeat.
4. **100 STEPS FARTLEK.** Run hard for 10 strides of one leg, then run slowly for 10. Repeat with 20, then 30, and so on. Once you hit 100, work your way back down.[2]

5. **ONE-TO-ONE.** Alternate between running 1 minute hard and 1 minute easy.[3]

6. **PLAYLIST FARTLEK.** Put an upbeat playlist on shuffle and run hard for the first minute of each song. Or do that for songs with a male vocalist and run at tempo effort for the first 2 minutes of a song with a female vocalist.[4]

7. **HILL FARTLEK.** On a rolling loop, run at tempo effort up each hill and recover on the downhills and flats.[5]

---

4 POPULAR INTERVAL WORKOUTS
(AND HOW TO RUN THEM RIGHT)

Interval workouts, which involve short, hard bursts of running followed by easy recovery periods,[6] have been helping runners get faster for decades. You can do them on a track, where each lap is usually 400 meters (about a quarter-mile), or elsewhere, if you have a GPS device or other way to measure distance. Warm up beforehand with at least a mile of easy jogging, and precede and follow interval days with either easy or rest days—because these will take it out of you.

1. **QUARTERS.** This is the old-school way of saying 400-meter repeats. You'll do at least four of them in a session—advanced runners might do up to 20!—with 200-meter walking or jogging recoveries in between. If you're doing fewer reps, try to hit 5K pace or slightly faster;[7] if you're on the higher end, 10K pace would be more appropriate.[8]

2. **800S (YASSO OR OTHERWISE).** These are twice as long as quarters, so you'll want twice as much recovery: 400 meters of walking or jogging. Aim for 5K to 10K pace, depending on how many reps you're doing—workouts may range from three or four all the way up to 10.[9] The exception is if you're running Yasso 800s to prepare for a marathon: You'll be working your way up to 10 reps and aiming to hit your marathon goal time, but in minutes and seconds instead of hours and minutes. For

example, if you want to run a 4:00:00 marathon, you should be able to do ten 4:00 800-meter reps.[10]

3. **MILE REPEATS.**[11] This is a tougher workout that's best for intermediate or advanced runners. Jog to recover for half the distance you've spent running hard, and your pace should match what you're training for (5K pace for up to three repeats for a 5K; 10K pace for up to five or six repeats for a 10K).

4. **PYRAMIDS.** These workouts involve starting with short reps (usually 200 or 400 meters), building to a long rep (about a mile), and then working your way back down.[12] Intermediate to advanced runners might do 400, 800, 1200, 1600, 1200, 800, 400. Newer runners might do 200, 400, 600, 800, 600, 400, 200. (Or you could do a progression that just climbs the pyramid, or one that starts at the top and descends.)[13] Jog or walk half the distance of the previous rep to recover and aim for about 5K pace.

> **BONUS TIP** Because 1 mile equals 1609.34 meters,[14] 400s and quarter-miles are basically interchangeable, as are half-miles and 800s and miles and 1600s. If you're on a track, meters are easier; if you're using a GPS watch that measures in miles, use those.

---

3 REASONS TO DO SPEEDWORK ON A TRACK . . . [15]

---

1. **YOU'LL RUN YOUR FASTEST.** When the terrain is flat and predictable, with just wide turns to contend with, your legs can turn over quickly and hit their top speeds. Bonus points if the track is rubberized and slightly bouncy.

2. **YOU'LL LEARN PERFECT PACING.** If you're aiming to hit a certain pace, a track allows you to check in regularly—every 100 to 200 meters, if you want—to ensure you're starting and staying at the right speed.

3. **ALL YOU NEED IS A STOPWATCH.** No fancy GPS devices

required here (though you can use one if you have it): One lap is 400 meters. Just bring something to keep time.

. . . AND 3 REASONS TO DO IT ELSEWHERE[16]

1. **YOU'LL BETTER MIMIC RACE-DAY CONDITIONS.** Most adults never compete on a track. You must learn to run fast on terrain similar to what you'll cover on race day: roads or possibly trails, with some climbs and descents.
2. **YOU AVOID FRETTING ABOUT ACCESS OR AN AUDIENCE.** A track that's open to the public can be hard to find. If you manage to locate one, you might be sharing with a lot of other runners, or with a team practicing on the infield.
3. **IT'S NOT SO FREAKIN' BORING.** One of the perks of outdoor running is that you get to explore new places and enjoy changing scenery. Not so on a track. If you're sick of running in ovals, practice being fast in a park, on a bike path, or somewhere else with no or minimal car traffic.

---

4 WAYS TO RECOVER DURING HARD WORKOUTS[17]

There's no one "right" way to recover when you're doing hill repeats or speedwork—which can be confusing for newbies. Here's a cheat sheet on what to do and when.

1. **STAND WHEN . . .** You're recovering from very short, very hard intervals or hill reps to build speed and strength. A combo of walking and standing is most effective—the key is to recover *completely* between reps, so you can give your all to each one. Just avoid doubling over, which can cause dizziness.
2. **WALK WHEN . . .** You're a newer runner who is doing repeats of 400 meters or longer. The break brings beginners' heart rates down, reduces impact, and provides a mental reprieve.

3. **JOG WHEN . . .** You're doing any speed session that doesn't involve all-out effort. Jogging keeps your heart rate up, builds endurance, and helps you learn to run hard on tired legs.

4. **KEEP PUSHING THE PACE WHEN . . .**[18] You're an advanced runner doing reps between 10K and half-marathon pace. Alternating between reps at that pace and "recoveries" at slightly slower than marathon pace teaches your body to use the metabolic by-products of hard exercise as fuel, which helps you excel in half or full marathons. Try 4 x 5:00 at 10 seconds faster than half-marathon pace with 5:00 recoveries at 10 seconds slower than marathon pace.

3 HIGH-INTENSITY INTERVAL WORKOUTS FOR TIME-STRAPPED ATHLETES

High-intensity interval training—or HIIT—has become a big trend, likely because this type of workout promises big benefits in a short amount of time. A HIIT workout usually involves alternating between short (10- to 60-second) but all-out work periods and recoveries that last one to four times as long.[19] The intensity, however, means a greater risk of injury, so do these workouts no more than once every 10 days and warm up super-thoroughly before each.[20]

1. **TRACK HIIT.**[21] Start with two 100-meter pickups (with 40 meters at top speed) with 2 to 3 minutes of recovery. Build to 6 x 150 meters (with 80 meters at top speed) with 3 or 4 minutes between each. Ultimately, you can work up to 10 repeats, increase the distance to 300 meters all-out, and/or shorten recoveries to just a minute.

2. **HILL HIIT.**[22] Start with three 30-second climbs at a comfortably hard effort and downhill walks for recovery. Build to 4 x 1:00 all-out climbs with a downhill jog (plus 30 to 60 seconds walking) to recover. Add reps, climb for up to 2 minutes, and/or tackle steeper hills as you progress.

28 | 205 TRAINING TIPS

3. **GYM HIIT.**[23] Start with a dynamic warmup: Spend 3 minutes cycling through 30 seconds each of moves like jumping jacks, inchworms, and hip swings—moves that increase your heart rate and flexibility without taxing your muscles much. Rest 1 minute, then alternate between three or four 6- to 9-minute exercise periods and 1-minute rest periods. During each exercise period, cycle through about three exercises, doing each for a minute at a time, incorporating leg, upper-body, and core work. For example, one period might include dumbbell rows (arms), circle lunges (legs), and planks (core).

---

3 TYPES OF *REALLY HARD* RUNNING (AND WHY TO DO EACH)[24]

Running all-out is something most grownups don't do often—but when you do, it's just so fun. Too much really hard running can lead to injury, however, so sprinkle small amounts into your routine. Try these types (after a thorough warmup, of course).

1. **SPRINTS.** You'll go as hard as you can without feeling out of control for 50 to 150 meters at a time. Recover completely with walking and jogging between each of 6 to 10 repetitions. You could sprint the straightaways and recover on the turns of a track, or just choose an approximately 100-meter length of trail or sidewalk to repeat.

2. **STRIDES.** These gradual pickups can cap off an easy run, as they help you shake off the soreness from a hard workout and prepare for future fast running. You'll do 8 to 10 reps of about 100 meters and walk for 30 to 60 seconds to recover. The first couple will build to about 5K pace at their peak; the last few can build to close to all-out.

3. **SURGES.** Adding a fast burst to the middle of a race can help you drop any opponents, but most of us only compete with ourselves. Still, learning to push and recover can help you endure hills or a too-fast start on race day. Try a fartlek run, one where

you surge to a point of your choosing ahead of you, jog until mostly recovered, and surge again.

THE 3 TYPES OF IN-BETWEEN RUNS (AND HOW THEY MAKE YOU FITTER)[25]

If it isn't speedwork, and it isn't long and easy, then what is it? "Tempo run" has become a kind of catchall for these in-between paces, and it can mean three different things, depending on who you're talking to.

1. **LACTATE-THRESHOLD RUNS.** When *Runner's World* mentions tempo runs, this is what we mean. Lactate-threshold pace is the fastest pace you can hold for about an hour. You start to slow when lactate, a metabolic by-product of exercise, accumulates in your blood faster than your body can clear it. (While lactate does not cause fatigue, it builds up in tandem with by-products that do.) When you run at this pace, you're training your body to hold the fastest speed at which your blood lactate levels stay fairly steady for a longer period of time. You'll know you're running the right pace if you can only speak in short phrases. Hold it for 20 to 30 minutes between a warmup and cooldown of 10 to 15 minutes each.

2. **RACE-PACE RUNS.** These are important if you're training for a fast half or full marathon: You want to learn the pace you're hoping to hold on race day and to practice taking in fuel at that harder-than-easy pace. Every 2 to 3 weeks, sub out your long, easy run for a long run with segments at race pace. Half marathoners should do 6 to 8 miles at race pace

> **BONUS TIP** If you find lactate-threshold or race-pace runs daunting, try inserting jogging breaks that last a minute or two after every mile (or between every few). You'll reap similar benefits without as much physical or mental stress.[26]

(between warmup and cooldown miles), while full marathoners should do 6 to 14 miles at pace.

3. **PROGRESSION RUNS.** You'll learn to run fast on tired legs and to meter your effort by gradually picking up the pace throughout the course of a progression run. After a 15-minute warmup, spend 30 minutes speeding up ever-so-slightly (by 10 to 15 seconds per mile) every 6 minutes until you hit threshold pace for the last 6 minutes. Cool down for 5 or 10 minutes.

4 COOLDOWNS THAT WILL MAKE YOU FITTER AND FASTER[27]

The word "cooldown" isn't a big part of many runners' vocabularies. You might do a little easy jogging after a speed workout or race, but you likely think of it as something you can bail on if you decide you don't feel like it. Well, don't! Continuing to exercise when you're fatigued can boost efficiency and mental toughness—all without adding another workout to your week. Try these variations.

1. **A FEW MORE MILES.** Thirty to 45 minutes of easy running after a speed workout or short (5K to 10K) tune-up race teaches your body to manage its fuel reserves more efficiently, which can help you avoid bonking when you go longer.

2. **A TEMPO FINISH.** After a short, hard speed workout (think: 200- to 400-meter repeats), do a couple laps at tempo pace before downshifting to easy pace. This requires your body to convert lactic acid into glucose it can use—an essential skill for maintaining a challenging pace like half-marathon pace for an extended period of time.

3. **SOME STRENGTH MOVES.** Do 5 to 10 minutes of bodyweight exercises like squats, burpees, and lunges (10 to 15 of each with 30 seconds of rest between) after tempo efforts. You'll build fast-twitch muscle your body can use when its slow-twitch muscles fatigue.

4. SOME 5K-PACE STRIDES. After running at half- or full-marathon pace, do five 20- to 30-second strides with full recovery (60 to 90 seconds of jogging). This is another way to engage and develop fast-twitch muscles.

FIVE

GOING LONGER

THE 3-STEP PLAN FOR PERFECT LONG RUNS[1]

Running for at least 90 minutes on a weekly basis increases aerobic capacity, strengthens your musculoskeletal system, and builds resolve: The ability to press on even when you're tired, bored, or both is what makes a good runner great. To make the most of these long slogs, here's what to do . . .

1. **BEFORE.** Have a 300- to 600-calorie meal that's mostly carbohydrates about 2 hours prior to departing, plus 17 to 20 ounces of water or sports drink. Keep sipping water as you assemble your midrun fuel, apply antichafing balm and sunscreen, and get dressed.

2. **DURING.** Start slow and stay slow. You should be able to pass the "talk test"—breathing easily enough to have a conversation—even if you're running solo. Start taking in calories after about 45 minutes. You'll want about 30 to 60 grams of carbohydrates per hour. As you fatigue, think "run tall" and "light stride" to stay upright and avoid shuffling.

3. **AFTER.** Have a glass of water ASAP. Within 30 minutes or so, refuel. You'll want 300 to 400 calories with a carb-to-protein

ratio of 3 or 4 to 1. Try to keep moving: Do some foam rolling, take a shower, and go on a walk to reduce postrun soreness.

5 WAYS TO AVOID POST-LONG-RUN KNOCKOUT[2]

Follow the aforementioned rules and you're on your way to feeling about as good as possible after your week's biggest run. But sometimes "as good as possible" won't cut it—the day of a party full of shrieking children, for example, or when you need to stay awake through something long and quiet, like a wedding ceremony. In those cases, try these tactics.

1. **START WELL-RESTED.** You'll feel extra zapped by a long run if you're tired before you even begin. Either go to bed earlier or sleep in later to get a full night's rest before heading out.
2. **DO IT LATER.** Most long runs should take place about when you'll be running on race day, usually the morning, but if you have conflicting obligations, you may start in the afternoon. That way, there are fewer hours between you and your pillow postrun. One caveat is that it can be more tempting to bail on long runs the longer you wait to do them.
3. **SPLIT IT UP.** Once in a while, you may run half of your long run in the morning and the other half later to conserve energy. Again—not a good tactic if you doubt you'll get back out there to complete it.
4. **MAYBE TAKE THAT ICE BATH AFTERWARD.** The jury's out on whether these should be a regular part of your routine, but nothing says "wake up!" like a tub full of freezing cold water. Combine it with coffee for an extra jolt.
5. **SWITCH DAYS.** Occasionally moving your long run to a Friday morning before work can ensure you feel fresh on both Saturday and Sunday. However, don't expect to have your most productive workday after an hours-long run that began at dawn.

HOW TO ENDURE 3 LONG-RUN PROBLEMS . . . ³

The number of things that can go wrong during a run increases exponentially with each mile you plan to log, which is why marathons are so freakin' hard to master. Here's how to cope with what might arise the next time you plan to be out there for longer than usual.

1. **GASTROINTESTINAL DISTRESS.** Up to 50 percent of endurance athletes deal with some variety of nausea at some point. The only way to solve an intestinal problem is to find a bathroom (or a private clump of woods) ASAP. Stomach sloshing, counterintuitively, could be caused by dehydration or an electrolyte imbalance: Take a walk break and have a few sips of water or sports drink. If you can't stop dry heaving, throwing up, or pooping, bail on the run.

2. **TERRIBLE WEATHER.** Skip or reschedule a run only if going outside is dangerous—that means strong winds, lightning, ice, or extreme heat—or if you're not training to race. Powering

through a downpour or a warmer-than-ideal day can prep you for the possibility of similar conditions on race day.

3. **EXHAUSTED LEGS.** It's normal to feel wiped out once in a while, especially if you're building up mileage before a race. Avoid out-and-back routes on these days and plan to repeat a short loop so you can bail if need be. Try slowing your pace, walking a bit, or taking a gel with water to resuscitate your legs. If you're still feeling fatigued 15 minutes after fueling, call it quits. You can try again the next day if you don't want to skip the miles.

. . . AND HOW TO PREVENT EACH IN THE FUTURE[4]

1. **GASTROINTESTINAL DISTRESS.** Whether you feel like you're about to erupt out of your mouth or your butt, something you consumed in the 48 hours leading up to the run or during the run could be to blame. Take stock of anything new or unusual and ban it for future long runs.

2. **TERRIBLE WEATHER.** Check the forecast each Thursday—if your planned long-run day (Saturday or Sunday) looks iffy, move it to the other weekend day or even Friday.

3. **EXHAUSTED LEGS.** Figure out what's causing the fatigue; if it's not high mileage, look to your sleep habits, what you've been eating, whether you've been drinking enough, and how you're feeling (sick? stressed?) when you're not running. If you can't pinpoint the cause of ongoing fatigue, see your doc—it could be anemia, a thyroid issue, or something else that requires treatment.

SIX

HILL TRAINING

4 TACTICS TO HELP YOU HATE HILLS LESS

Climbing never gets easier—you just get a little bit faster. It takes most runners 10 to 20 percent more energy to run inclines than to run flats.[1] But as 1972 Olympic marathon gold medalist Frank Shorter once said, "Hills are speedwork in disguise."[2] They're worth doing *because* they're hard. If you're struggling mightily, try these fast fixes.

1. **ADJUST YOUR FORM.** When climbing, take short, quick steps, pushing off from your toes. Avoid slumping forward at the waist or from your shoulders, and swing your arms to help propel yourself.[3]

2. **METER YOUR EFFORT.** If what you hate about hills is how they make you huff and puff, there's a simple solution: Slow down. Pay attention to the rhythm of your breathing on flats and try to match it as you climb.[4] If that means slowing significantly, or even taking walk breaks, so be it—your body responds to effort, not pace.

3. **REFRAME YOUR FOES.** Some runners get a mental boost

HELLO THERE, BUDDY

out of naming the most grueling hills they encounter (e.g., "Hello, Cardiac Climb. We meet again."). Others find it helpful to think of inclines in a positive light; that is, as friends instead of enemies. For example, Chicago-based running coach Jenny Hadfield borrowed her hill-climbing mantra from a mountain-climbing expedition in which the guide told the group to "be the mountain"—to work with it instead of against it.[5] The more mental and physical energy you burn fighting the climb, the less you'll have to spare to actually climb it.

BONUS TIP Downhill running improves your turnover, which may, in turn, help you run faster.[7] It is hard on your body, though, so tread carefully. Try doing sets of two to four downhill repeats at a comfortably hard pace on a gentle slope (2 to 3 percent grade) no more than every other week.[8] If you can find a soft surface such as grass, dirt, or gravel, your body will thank you.

> **BONUS TIP** If you don't mind looking a little wacky, just run with high knees on flat ground: You'll use the form and recruit the muscles you'd use on a real incline. Start with 30-second bursts midrun and make sure to pump your arms and land softly as you "climb."[13]

4. REPEAT (OR DON'T). While hill repeats make for a great workout, you don't have to do them if you dread them. Instead, plan a route that hits a variety of inclines of various lengths and steepnesses. If you're training for something, this better mimics what you'll experience on race day anyway.[6]

4 PLACES FLATLANDERS CAN CLIMB

"But there are no hills near me!" This excuse is BS, because surely you can find one of these alternatives within running (or driving) distance.

1. **PARKING GARAGES.** Time your workout for an off-peak hour to avoid exhaust as well as drivers that may not be expecting to see runners.[9]

2. **OVERPASSES/BRIDGES.** Stick to ones with pedestrian-friendly sidewalks and maybe leave your hat or visor at home on windy days—you'll get the worst gusts here.

3. **STAIRS.** Stairs are much steeper than most hills, so they'll really work your legs and lungs.[10] After warming up for 10 minutes, try a workout that involves 20 to 30 seconds of climbing at a comfortably hard effort followed by an equal amount of time descending at an easier effort.[11] (A stadium is a great place to do this.)

4. **THE TREADMILL.** Just about every machine allows you to climb, while some allow you to climb *and* descend. Whenever you hit the 'mill—even for an easy run—vary the belt between a 1 percent decline and 1.5 percent incline to engage different muscles and more accurately mimic the demands of outdoor running.[12]

SEVEN

HANDLING EXTREME WEATHER

THE 8 RULES OF TRAINING IN THE HEAT . . . [1,2]

Exercising in hot weather is tougher than doing it in the cold. You can always put on more layers, but—unless you're running through a nudist colony—you can only take off so many. It can also be pretty dangerous: Warm weather and exercise together can raise your body temperature sky-high and cause heat-related illnesses. Still, if you're careful, you can usually train outside safely.

1. **SLOW DOWN.** You simply won't be able to run as fast in heat, and that's okay. Instead, try to match duration and effort level. If an easy 5-miler takes you 50 minutes in good conditions, do an easy-effort 50-minute run in heat. For a speedwork example, swap 400s at 8:00 pace with 2:00 "on" reps and 1:00 jogging recoveries.

2. **PROTECT YOURSELF.** Wear a hat or visor, sunglasses, and sunscreen, even on overcast days.

3. **HYDRATE RIGHT.** "Drink when you're thirsty" is a good rule of thumb—carry a handheld bottle or wear a fuel belt to ensure fluid is available when you want it. You'll be losing a lot of salt in your sweat, so make sure to take in some electrolytes (via

gels, chews, or sports drink) if you're going long.

4. **CHILL OUT.** Ice is your friend. Stick it under your hat or in your sports bra. Soak a bandanna in water, stick it in the freezer, and loop it around your neck.

BONUS TIP If it's really hot, grab a foam noodle, jog 10 to 15 minutes to your local pool, remove your shirt and shoes, and hop in. Spend 20 minutes aqua-jogging with the noodle looped beneath your armpits, then get out and jog home. Refreshing![3]

5. **RUN LOOPS.** Now's not a good time for that out-and-back 20-miler. Plan a figure-eight loop or a series of short loops that double back to your house or car, where you can re-up on cold drinks and ice.

6. **TIME IT RIGHT.** It's cooler at or before dawn and at or after dusk. If you live somewhere truly beastly, these might be your best windows for running—just make sure you're visible by wearing lights and reflective clothing.

7. **KNOW WHEN TO GO INSIDE.** If the heat index tops 95°F, you'll get a better workout if you can do it on a treadmill in an air-conditioned room. If you really struggle in heat, your personal threshold might be lower. If you hate the treadmill, you can alternate between 5 to 10 minutes on it and 5 to 10 minutes outdoors.

8. **KNOW IT'S WORTH-WHILE.** Your body increases blood volume to cool itself during warm-weather running, which is why training feels extra difficult when it first gets hot.

BONUS TIP Caught in a thunderstorm? You're in danger if there are 5 or fewer seconds between thunderclaps and lightning flashes. Sprint to a nonmetallic building ASAP and get inside or under an awning. If you're truly in the middle of nowhere, crouch in a low-lying spot away from tall objects. Wait until you can no longer see lightning to resume your run.[4]

BONUS TIP Instead of dreading rainy runs, embrace them. Wear older shoes, a brimmed hat, and plenty of antichafing balm, and set out on a "splash run" that includes as many forceful jumps into big puddles as possible. You're going to get wet anyway—why not have fun with it?

Still, your blood stays supercharged for a few weeks after temperatures fall in autumn, when the surplus helps fuel working muscles. Slog through the summer and you'll feel like a million dollars when fall rolls around.

. . . AND THE 4 RULES OF HEAT ACCLIMATION[5,6]

If you ever want to run a late-spring race or a winter destination race somewhere warm, you'll be logging most of your miles in cold temps—which means extra misery if race day ends up being hot. Luckily, you can prep your body for warm conditions even if it's not warm where you live.

1. **RUN HOT.** This means either *really* bundling up for an outdoor run or hitting a treadmill in a warm room sans fan. The treadmill option is safer, as you'll have fluid on hand and are more likely to feel the urge to drink. You'll know it's hot enough to help if you feel uncomfortably warm.

2. **TIME IT RIGHT . . .** The effects of heat acclimation don't last forever, so do most of your sweaty runs during the 2 to 3 weeks prerace. Five to 10 hot runs—spaced no more than 3 days apart—is the goal.

3. **. . . BUT DON'T OVERDO IT.** You'll be heat-running during taper, so stick to an easy pace—even if that pace ends up being slower than your cool-weather easy pace. Runs of at least 60 minutes give you the most benefit, but every little bit counts.

4. **MAKE YOURSELF SWEAT.** Research shows that visiting a sauna or taking a hot bath postrun can boost blood volume, which is what helps you run better in heat. You'll need to keep your core temp elevated for at least 30 minutes to see results, but saunas can be a bit much if you're unaccustomed, so work your way up from 5- to 10-minute sessions. Employ this technique *only* after runs in cool temps—pairing it with a hot run could be dangerous.

THE 6 RULES OF WINTER TRAINING[7]

If you're running during the winter and it's not because you're in the starry-eyed first few days of pursuing a New Year's resolution, you're already better off than most people. Overcoming the urge to hibernate is a feat, especially if you live somewhere where it gets *really* dark, cold, snowy, and/or icy. Here's what to do to make the most of your winter training.

1. **BUNDLE UP (WITHIN REASON).** You should be a little bit chilly before you begin. Wear layers you can shed as you warm up and make sure you have pockets for a hat or pair of gloves.

2. **STAY VISIBLE.** This means blinking lights and reflective gear if it's not 100 percent light outside for your *entire* run.

3. **AVOID A WIPEOUT.** Find a clear, plowed route whenever possible. In fresh snow, slow way down, consider traction devices you can slip over your running shoes, and scan the horizon for shiny patches of ice.

> **BONUS TIP** A few sets of jumping jacks, walking lunges, and half-squats before you leave the house on a cool day can make venturing outside feel less jarring and reduce your risk of injury.[8]

4. **KNOW WHEN TO HEAD INDOORS.** Don't mess around with widespread ice, or with temps or windchills so low that weather services are issuing exposed-skin advisories. In these cases, just hit the treadmill. To make it less boring (and more similar to outdoor running), adjust the incline and pace frequently.

5. **SHIFT YOUR SCHEDULE.** If you're able to run at lunchtime—the warmest, brightest part of the day—do it! If you have a day job, pack wipes and deodorant to de-stink before heading back to work. And if you don't normally run on both weekend days, you may want to through the winter: Leaving a bit later in the morning is the cure for all the season's ills.

6. **DO THE MINIMUM.** Run at least 3 days per week (for at least 20 to 30 minutes at a time) to maintain some base fitness. That way, you'll be able to ramp up mileage when fair weather comes around.

7 TREADMILL SAFETY TIPS[9]

While treadmills are a great option when the weather outside is frightful, they can be tough for less coordinated runners. If you fall on a road run, all you have to contend with is gravity. If you fall on a treadmill . . . it can get ugly. To minimize your chances of a 'mill mishap, follow these steps.

1. **READ THE DIRECTIONS.** It's key to know how your machine works—and how to set it up and maintain it to avoid malfunctions.

2. **STAY FOCUSED.** Fiddling with your phone, your clothing, or your water bottle while the belt is moving is unwise. Get comfortable *before* you get going.

3. **START SLOWLY.** Stand on the belt before it begins moving. Increase your pace gradually, especially on a machine that's new to you—each one ramps up at a different rate.

4. **USE THE SAFETY FEATURES.** Most runners ignore the safety clip on a string that will stop the belt if you fly off. That's a recipe for a messed-up face. Others will leave the belt moving if they need to step off, which makes for a dangerous return. Instead, use the "pause" button.

5. **PREPARE FOR THE WORST.** Leave about 4 feet of space behind a home treadmill so, if you are forcefully ejected, you won't slam into something. Install a soft surface, like rubber matting or carpet, behind the machine for a gentler wipeout.

6. **KEEP YOURSELF IN CHECK . . .** Whenever you run all-out, it's smart to go only as fast as you can move while still feeling like you have control of your body—and it's doubly smart on a treadmill. When doing speedwork, limit your exertion to a 9 on a scale of 1 to 10.

7. **. . . AND KIDS AND PETS AWAY.** Unsupervised children can really hurt themselves on a treadmill, so keep it in a place they can't easily access. And if a curious dog or cat wanders onto or near a moving belt without your realizing it, that's bad news for you *and* your fuzzy friend.

EIGHT

RACE TRAINING

PREDICTOR WORKOUTS FOR
4 RACE DISTANCES[1]

If you want to know how fast you'll finish your next race, you can either visit a psychic or try one of these workouts. The workouts are free, so they're probably your best bet. Do yours once, 3 to 5 weeks before race day, after an adequate warmup (10 to 15 minutes of jogging, dynamic stretches, and a few strides).

1. **5K.** Run 5 x 1K at 5K effort with a 400-meter recovery jog between each. Take the average of your 1K times and multiply by 5 to estimate your race time.
2. **10K.** Run 5 x 1 mile at 10K effort with a 400-meter recovery jog between each. Take the average of your mile times and multiply by 6.2 to estimate your race time.
3. **HALF MARATHON.** Run a 10K at 80 percent effort. Then take your finishing time in minutes (59:30 becomes 59.5, for example), add .93, and multiply by 2.11 to estimate your race time.
4. **FULL MARATHON.** Run marathon pace for 10 to 14 miles of a 20-mile long run. The average pace for those miles is about what you'll be able to sustain on race day, if you've trained properly and tapered.

HOW TO EXECUTE 3 PERFECT TAPER WEEKS . . . [2]

After you hit peak mileage in half- or full-marathon training, you spend a few weeks before the race winding down and resting up—a period known as the taper. Whether you despise the taper or count down the days until it begins, doing it right sets you up for peak performance. Here's how.

1. **THREE WEEKS UNTIL RACE DAY.** Drop your weekly mileage by about 25 percent by shortening each run and maintaining the same frequency. If you've been doing speedwork, tempo runs, or race-pace work, keep shorter versions of those on the schedule—you want your legs to continue to practice turning over.

2. **TWO WEEKS UNTIL RACE DAY.** Cut your miles back another 15 to 25 percent. (If you prefer to do a 2-week taper—so your highest mileage week was last week—drop mileage by 30 to 40 percent this week.) Just because you're running less doesn't mean you need to drastically alter your diet. Instead, prioritize fruits, veggies, and whole grains to stay fueled and healthy.

3. **ONE WEEK UNTIL RACE DAY.** Stop thinking about mileage and just do a few 25- to 30-minute runs. A few days before the event, practice hitting race pace, in *very* short bursts, to keep legs fresh. (For example, marathoners might run 5 x 1K at race pace with 2:00 recovery.) Continue doing whatever dynamic stretches or mobility drills you did throughout training to preserve flexibility and range of motion.

. . . AND HOW TO TRAIN IN THE 5 WEEKS FOLLOWING YOUR GOAL RACE[3]

Remember the taper? (Of course you do—we just talked about it!) The best way to ease back into running after a half or full marathon is what's known as a "reverse taper"—that is, more or less doing what you did leading up to the race, but backward. Here's how.

1. **THE WEEK AFTER THE RACE.** Take a break from running. Walking and/or low-impact, easy-effort cross-training is encouraged—you'll get blood flowing to beat-up muscles and promote a faster recovery.
2. **WEEK 2.** Run easy every other day, logging about 20 to 30 percent of your peak week's mileage.
3. **WEEK 3.** You may run up to half of your previous peak mileage, but all at an easy pace.
4. **WEEK 4.** You may run 90 to 100 percent of your previous mileage, but again, keep it all slow and comfortable. (And there's nothing wrong with easing back in more slowly, especially if you have some time before beginning your next training cycle. You've earned a break!)
5. **WEEK 5 AND ON.** Now you can bring back some quality work (speedwork, tempo runs)—but you don't have to unless you're planning to race again soon.

THE 3 RULES OF TRAINING BETWEEN TRAINING CYCLES[4]

The period between finishing one race and starting to train for another can be confusing. Without a day-by-day plan to turn to for guidance, some runners end up running too much (or too little) and heading into their next cycle at a disadvantage. But fear not: If you follow these guidelines, you'll set yourself up for success after success.

1. **ERR ON THE SIDE OF MORE REST.** After a half, take 1 to 3 weeks off; after a full, 2 to 4. If you were racing for fun, you can rest less; if you pushed to your limits, you'll need more. Fill the time with low-impact cross-training such as lower-body strength work, swimming, cycling, or pool running.

2. **EASE BACK IN.** For the first postbreak week, do three or four easy runs of 3 or 4 miles each, taking a nonrunning day between each. The next week, run the same number of days you plan to run in your next training cycle, all short and easy. Gradually bump up mileage (adding a mile to each run every fourth week or so) so your volume matches that of the first week of your next training plan by the end of your maintenance phase. Resume long runs (25 to 30 percent of your weekly mileage) 3 to 4 weeks postbreak.

3. **KEEP INTENSITY LOW.** All your miles should be easy for the first 3 to 4 postbreak weeks. Then you can add five to ten strides (on flat ground or uphill) during or after three runs per week. That's it: Don't race or do any other hard workouts, as you'll be doing them soon enough to prep for your next event.

4 TRAINING STRATEGIES TO PREPARE YOU FOR AN OVERNIGHT RELAY[5]

If spending the bulk of 2 days (including a full night) inside a van with several other sweaty runners sounds like fun to you, you're not alone: Overnight relays (like the Ragnar series) are popular, if challenging to train for. If you function well on limited sleep, that's a huge advantage—because you'll only manage a few hours on relay weekend—but you also have to prepare for the running.

1. **NAIL THE LONG RUN.** You'll know which legs you're doing in advance, and they'll all be different lengths and levels of difficulty. Log at least 2 long runs that match the length (and, if possible, hilliness) of your longest leg, completing the last long run about 2 weeks from race day.

2. **ADD DOUBLES.** Events like Ragnar require you to run 3 times in 2 days. If you're only running every other day, start by running 2 consecutive days once per week. Then shift those runs close together—for example, run Tuesday night and Wednesday morning. As the race draws nearer, plan three consecutive

weekends featuring two-a-days (one run in the morning and one in the afternoon or evening), keeping the pace easy on at least the first run.

3. **DO SOME NIGHT RUNS.** Test your reflective gear and lights for fit and comfort before race day. If you can, head out with one or more of your teammates—they'll need to prep too, and there's safety in numbers.

4. **WORK ON PACE.** Most runners end up completing relay legs somewhere between half-marathon and 10K pace. Practice some running around that pace in training, including a mile or two of it at the end of your second two-a-day run if possible, to get used to running harder when you're tired.

7 FIRST-TIMERS' TRIATHLON TRAINING TIPS

Many runners become runners because they're not so good at other sports. (Cut from the soccer or football or field hockey team? Try cross-country!) But the multisport training required to prep for a triathlon busts boredom and makes you a more well-rounded athlete—if you can manage it without drowning or breaking your body in a spectacular cycling wipeout. Here's how runners can get ready to swim and bike.

1. **MEET THE MINIMUM.** Before signing up for a tri of any distance, you should be comfortable swimming 50 meters (one lap of a pool) and riding for 30 minutes without stopping. Once you're there, target a sprint-distance tri (quarter-mile swim, 12-mile ride, 5K run) at least 6 weeks in the future.

2. **KNOW WHAT YOU'RE GETTING INTO.** Because you have to train for three sports, you'll likely be working out 5 or 6 days per week: two swims, two or three bike rides, and two or three runs. Some days, you'll do "brick" workouts that start with a bike ride and finish with a run.

3. **FIND A TRAINING PLAN.** You don't want to wing it when two fairly new-to-you disciplines are involved. Look for a plan that includes drills to help you improve your swim and bike techniques. See runnersworld.com/trainingplans for some options.

4. **WHEN IN DOUBT, TAKE A SWIM LESSON.** Swimming is all about technique. You'll be able to go faster and farther with less effort if you're doing it right, and you can't be sure you're doing it right without eyes on you as you swim.

5. **BE YOUR OWN MECHANIC.** One reason running is so appealing is that mechanical malfunctions are rare. Unless your sole falls off your shoe midrun, not much can go seriously wrong gear-wise. Not so on a bike. Ask a friend, a bike mechanic, or YouTube to teach you how to change a flat, then practice at home.

6. **REVAMP YOUR RUNNING.** Because you'll be getting plenty of aerobic conditioning from easy swims and bike rides, you should be running harder than easy when you do run. The exception is when you're running after a bike ride in a "brick" workout. Then start with short, easy runs and work up to one or two moderate-effort postride runs.

7. **MIMIC THE COURSE (ESPECIALLY THE SWIM).** If you do all your swim training in a pool, you might panic in the murky, nonchlorinated water you're likely to encounter on race day. Many tris begin in a lake, so do at least a couple practice swims there to decrease your fear of the unknown.

---

6 FIRST-TIMERS' OBSTACLE-RACE TRAINING TIPS[6]

If all your friends are doing a Tough Mudder or Spartan Race and you want to join them—or they threaten to forever brand you a wimp if you don't sign up—this is for you. Your existing running fitness already provides a good base, but here are some suggestions to try to increase your chances of finishing without some kind of running-derailing injury.

1. **MOVE YOUR WEEKLY LONG RUNS TO TRAILS.** Many obstacle races are held on farms or ski slopes, on terrain riddled with holes and rocks. If you're new to trails, start with 5 miles; if you're not, start with your usual long-run distance. Keep a conversational pace, even if that means running more slowly than you would on roads.

2. **BREAK UP YOUR LONG RUNS WITH UPPER-BODY STRENGTH WORK.** After 5 to 10 minutes of running, drop and do 10 pushups; 5 to 10 minutes later, do 15 burpees. This simulates the run, conquer-obstacle, run pattern you'll experience on race day—and shores up your arms, shoulders, and back, which, if you're like most runners, are all underdeveloped.

3. **ADD TRACK WORKOUTS.** To mimic the hard running you'll do between obstacles, every 2 weeks, do 400-meter repeats at a comfortably hard pace. At the end of each repeat, jump rope for 30 seconds, then recover with 2 minutes of walking. Start with five repeats; add one each workout until you hit eight.

4. **BUILD LOWER-BODY POWER WITH HILL SPRINTS . . .** Once a week, jog for at least 10 minutes to a slope that feels

steep (about a 10 percent grade), then do 5 repeats: Run all-out uphill for 10 seconds, then walk downhill and around the base until your breathing fully recovers (at least 90 seconds). Add a rep each week until you reach 12.

5. **. . . AND DON'T FORGET THE DOWNHILLS.** Descending can be hard on your quads—but you'll still have to do a good amount of it on race day. To prepare, head to a hill of the same steepness as the one you sprint up—preferably one that's grassy or otherwise softer than roads. Do ten 10-second downhill repeats at a moderate effort, then walk back up to recover. Add two reps each week until you reach 20.

6. **PREP FOR SPECIFIC OBSTACLES AS MUCH AS POSSIBLE.** You may not be able to find Dumpsters filled with ice water or live wires that give you mild electric shocks for prerace-day practice—why did you sign up for this torture, again?—but do what you can. If you know you'll need to bear-crawl under wire, bear-crawl around your house. If you know you'll be jumping from something high into water, hit the diving board at your pool. Specificity of training is important, even when you're training for something crazy.

SECTION 2

193 NUTRITION TIPS

THE 5 GOLDEN RULES OF NUTRITION

1. **"EAT FOOD. NOT TOO MUCH. MOSTLY PLANTS."** This rule comes from author and activist Michael Pollan (*In Defense of Food*), and there's no better way to sum up what most nutritionists and dietitians agree upon: Real food—the stuff you find on the perimeter of the grocery store—beats packaged, processed food. At meals, eat until you're satisfied, not stuffed. And most of what you eat, about half of your plate at every meal,[1] should be fruits, veggies, and legumes.

2. **LEAVE SOME WIGGLE ROOM.** If you eat healthily about 80 percent of the time, that's good enough to fuel your workouts and foster overall wellness.[2]

3. **HYDRATE.** Drink a glass of water after you get up in the morning[3] and have more H_2O when you're thirsty.[4] Sports drinks are generally unnecessary—except on very hot days, when the electrolytes can help you absorb the fluid better, and on long runs, when you may need the calories.[5]

4. **EAT BEFORE (AND DURING) LONG OR HARD RUNS.** You can skip prerun fuel if you're going easy for less than an hour

and you don't feel hungry.[6] Have an easy-to-digest meal or snack that's high in simple carbohydrates before more intense efforts. On long runs, take in 30 to 60 grams of carbs each hour after your first hour.[7]

5. **KNOW WHEN TO CARBO-LOAD.** Put down the pasta, 5K runners: You only need to carbo-load before races that will last 2 or more hours. That doesn't mean eating whole loaves of crusty Italian bread in one sitting, either—shift your diet so that more of your calories come from carbs in the days leading up to your event.[8]

NINE

FUELING YOUR RUNS

---

3 WAYS TO TELL IF YOU'RE
PROPERLY HYDRATED

There are a few reasons prerace porta-potty lines are so long. Number one (yuk, yuk) is that it's important to adequately hydrate before, during, and after exertion, as water is necessary for every metabolic process in your body—including those that help you run.[1] Finding your personal sweet spot is important: If you're severely dehydrated, you may succumb to heat illness upon exertion, even on not-so-hot days,[2] while extreme overhydration can cause a dangerous condition called hyponatremia, which can lead to severe illness and even death.[3] But striking the right balance isn't hard if you know what to look for.

1. **BEFORE A RUN: THE PEE TEST.** If you're properly hydrated, your urine should be pale yellow—roughly the color of lemonade. Darker urine means "drink up"; lighter means "enough already!"[4]

2. **DURING A RUN: THE THIRST TEST.** Generally, your own thirst is a good indicator of how much fluid you need to consume on a run.[5] If it's especially warm out, take in a gulp of

water or sports drink about every 20 minutes, but listen to your body: If your stomach feels sloshy, drink less until it feels normal again.[6]

3. **AFTER A RUN: THE SWEAT TEST.** To find out exactly how much you need to drink, weigh yourself nude before and after a 60-minute run. The amount of weight you lose equals how much fluid you need per hour (1 pound equals 16 ounces of fluid) in that day's weather conditions. If you drank during the run, subtract that amount from your hourly sweat rate.[7]

7 HYDRATION MYTHS—BUSTED![8]

You've probably heard some hydration-related nonsense over the years—that you should drink eight glasses of water per day, for example—and we're here to tell you what's true.

1. **THERE'S NO PERFECT AMOUNT OF WATER TO DRINK PER DAY.** Fluid needs vary from person to person and even from day to day. Generally, if you're thirsty, you should drink. If you're not, you're probably good.

2. **CAFFEINE WON'T CAUSE DEHYDRATION.** If you have a small amount (two cups of coffee or less), you may urinate a bit more for a few hours, but running could delay that effect. Research suggests that, because exercise diverts blood flow to working muscles and away from your kidneys, you may not feel the diuretic effects until after you run.

3. **THIRST IS A GOOD INDICATOR OF HOW MUCH TO DRINK MIDRUN.** The one reason you might want to drink before you're thirsty is that you only have access to fluids every few miles, such as when you pass water fountains or aid stations. Even then, tread carefully, because . . .

4. **DRINKING TOO MUCH CAN BE JUST AS DANGEROUS AS DRINKING TOO LITTLE.** Chug too much water and you'll dilute the sodium levels in your blood, which can cause a condition called hyponatremia. Symptoms include nausea, vomit-

ing, headache, and, in extreme cases, seizures.[9] Meanwhile, mild dehydration won't hurt your health or your performance.

5. **PURE WATER ISN'T ALWAYS BEST.** If you're going long in hot weather, you'll lose salt as you sweat. You need to replace that salt to be able to absorb the fluids you're taking in, so have some sports drink or other fuel containing electrolytes along the way.

6. **"DETOXING" IS BULLSHIT.** Your body cleanses itself naturally; you don't need a ton of fluids to "flush out toxins." The only people who should be drinking more water to improve kidney function are those who've had kidney stones. If you haven't, eat and drink like a normal human.

7. **PROPER HYDRATION ALONE WON'T PREVENT HEAT-STROKE.** It's true that dehydration raises your risk of heat-related illnesses like heatstroke (identified by a body temperature higher than 104°F). But factors like how fit you are, how intensely you're exercising, and external variables like air temperature and humidity also play a role. While it's true that you need to hydrate on hot days, you also need to take it down a notch—see "The 8 Rules of Training in the Heat" (page 40) for further instruction.

16 EASY-TO-DIGEST PRERUN SNACKS (FROM LEAST CALORIC TO MOST)[10]

If you're running for up to 60 minutes, take in up to 200 calories beforehand. For longer runs, you'll want more than 200 calories in advance, plus some on-the-run carbs. Foods containing fat (nut butters), protein (dairy and meat), or fiber (whole grains and veggies) take more time to digest than simple carbs, but they also keep you sated longer. Have heavier snacks 60 to 90 minutes before you head out.

1. 3 graham cracker squares with 1 teaspoon honey (98 calories)
2. 16-ounce sports drink (125 calories)

3. 1 cup berries with ½ cup low-fat cottage cheese (160 calories)
4. 1 cup low-fiber cereal with ½ cup fat-free milk (195 calories)
5. 2 fig bar cookies (200 calories)
6. 1 medium banana and 1 tablespoon nut butter (200 calories)
7. 2 ounces honey–whole wheat pretzels dipped in 1 tablespoon natural peanut butter (230 calories)
8. 1 cup apple-cinnamon oat cereal with 1 cup fat-free milk and 1 medium banana (255 calories)
9. ½ cup steel-cut oats with fat-free milk, topped with 1 cup sliced strawberries (256 calories)
10. 2 ounces pretzels with 2 tablespoons hummus (263 calories)
11. 2 whole grain waffles (frozen) with 2 tablespoons maple syrup (270 calories)
12. 3 ounces deli turkey wrapped in a flour tortilla with 1 cup shredded veggies (275 calories)
13. 6 ounces low-fat fruit yogurt and 1 medium peach (275 calories)
14. Peanut butter and banana sandwich on whole grain bread (360 calories)
15. 1 bagel with 1 tablespoon nut butter and 1 tablespoon jam or honey (390 calories)
16. 15 animal crackers dipped in 2 tablespoons peanut butter (390 calories)

6 EVERYDAY FOODS YOU CAN USE AS MIDRUN FUEL

When you're running for longer than about 75 minutes, you need to take in easily digestible carbs midrun (30 to 60 grams per hour) to prevent bonking: When your body and mind run low on energy, you become sluggish and cranky.[11] There are many products designed for this purpose, but if you don't have any—or if you'd prefer to use something that's already in your pantry—try one of these.

1. **HONEY.** It's nature's Gu. Carrying a full bear-shaped bottle isn't practical, but many fast-food restaurants offer packets or dipping

cups of the sweet stuff.[12]
Each half-ounce packet
contains 43 calories and
12 grams of carbs.[13]

BONUS TIP Warm a midrun gel in your pocket, waistband, or sports bra before you eat it—it'll thin and go down easier. (Do the same to soften gummy fuel you chew when it's cold outside.)[15]

2. **MAPLE SYRUP.** It's, um, nature's *other* Gu.[14] Solve the portability problem by putting some into a small, handheld water bottle. Two tablespoons have about 100 calories and 26 grams of carbs, about the same amount in a standard gel.[16]

3. **JELLY PACKS.** Grab a handful the next time you're enjoying breakfast at a diner. Each one has about 13 grams of carbs.[17]

4. **FIG BAR COOKIES.** One of these cookies will net you 20 grams of carbs and 100 calories.[18]

5. **CANDY.** Swedish Fish, jelly beans, and gumdrops are popular, easy-to-chew options.[19]

6. **MINI PRETZELS.** If you can't take any more sweet midrun fuel, tiny pretzels are a great option.[20] They are, however, less calorically dense than sugary fuels (with 35 grams of carbs in a cup),[21] so unless you plan to carry a backpack full of them, it's smart to make them just one part of your fueling plan.

---

10 TOTALLY SOLID POSTRUN RECOVERY SNACKS[22]

The need to refuel after a workout is a good excuse for adults to drink chocolate milk, but sugary moo juice isn't your only option. To support muscle recovery after a speed workout or long run, take in 150 to 300 calories of carbs and protein within an hour or so.[23] The ratio of carbs to protein should be between 2:1 and 4:1.[24] These options, from least caloric to most, fit the bill.

1. 1 whole wheat slice of toast topped with 1 scrambled egg and 2 tablespoons salsa: 185 calories, 2:1 ratio

2. 1 packet flavored oatmeal made with $\frac{1}{2}$ cup low-fat milk: 187 calories, 4:1 ratio
3. Small apple with 1 ounce cheddar cheese: 190 calories, 3:1 ratio
4. 1 cup plain, low-fat yogurt mixed with 1 cup raspberries: 218 calories, 2:1 ratio
5. 1 whole wheat slice of toast with 1 tablespoon peanut butter and 1 tablespoon jam: 219 calories, 4:1 ratio
6. Small sandwich (3 slices deli meat on 2 slices whole wheat bread) plus 1 cup grapes: 238 calories, 3:1 ratio
7. Small banana with 1 $\frac{1}{2}$ tablespoons peanut butter: 240 calories, 4:1 ratio
8. Small cinnamon-raisin bagel with 1 tablespoon cashew butter: 250 calories, 4:1 ratio
9. 12 ounces low-fat chocolate milk: 266 calories, 4:1 ratio
10. Smoothie (1 cup fat-free milk, 1 large banana, 1 scoop protein powder): 280 calories, 2:1 ratio

THE 6 RULES OF CARBO-LOADING

Imagining feasting on a heap of pasta the night before their goal race might help some runners through their longest, hardest training. However, most of us don't carbo-load properly, which can lead to subpar performance—and, possibly, a lot of time in the bathroom race morning. Here's how to do it right.

1. **KNOW WHEN TO BOTHER.** The purpose of carbo-loading is to fill your body's stores of glycogen, the fuel in your muscles that's easiest to burn for energy.[25] If you're running a 5K or 10K, however, your normal diet will do[26]—so cancel that reservation at the Italian buffet.

2. **DON'T OVERDO IT.** The aforementioned pasta pile is a bad idea—a single, over-the-top prerace dinner is one way to make yourself poop, *a lot*, the next morning. Instead, start carbo-loading 2 or 3 days before the race and don't consume *more* calories than usual—just take in a greater proportion of them

(85 to 95 percent) from easily digested carbs.[27]

3. **CHOOSE WISELY.**[28] Now's not the time for high-fiber, whole wheat bread. Good options include rice, tortillas, white bread, juice, pancakes, waffles, bagels, bananas, and baked potatoes (sans skin). Fat and protein take longer to digest than carbs, so limit them—top toast with jam instead of butter or nut butter, and pasta with marinara sauce instead of pesto or cream sauce.

> **BONUS TIP** Know what your goal race is serving on the course: Some trendy sports drinks provide only electrolytes (not calories), so if you rely on Gatorade or Powerade as midrun fuel, you might be out of luck if the event is sponsored by a low- or no-cal drink. It's always wise to BYO fuel, anyway, so you're guaranteed to have stuff that sits well.

4. **PEEL YOUR FRUITS.** You can still eat high-fiber options like apples and pears *if* you remove the most fibrous part: the skin.[29]

5. **MAYBE DON'T WEIGH YOURSELF.** This process could make you heavier—we're talking 4 or more pounds heavier—but that's because your body stores water as it stores glycogen.[30] Weigh yourself if you want proof you're doing it right, but if that number will freak you out, stow the scale until after the race.

6. **TRY IT IN TRAINING.**[31] Do what you'll do before race day in the days leading up to your longest training run. This will help you get a sense of what does and doesn't agree with you before the stakes are higher.

---

6 STRATEGIES TO AVOID BONKING, HITTING THE WALL, OR WHATEVER YOU WANT TO CALL IT

It can happen during longer runs and races: You're chugging along, feeling somewhere between "fine" and "great," and then suddenly, you are *not* okay. Your legs feel leaden, you slow noticeably, and no matter how hard you try, you cannot will yourself to think anything more positive than "this really sucks." Prevent this catastrophe with these tips.

1. **UNDERSTAND WHY THIS HAPPENS.** Your muscles and your brain run their best on carbohydrates. When they don't get enough—either from what you're taking in before or during a run, or from what's stored as glycogen in your body—you bonk.

2. **KNOW HOW TO ID IT.** A true bonk affects your legs *and* your brain—you may feel cranky, despondent, belligerent, or otherwise "off" mentally. If only your legs are tired and sore, you may simply be undertrained for the distance you're attempting.

3. **FIND A CARB SOURCE YOU LIKE . . .** This is essential only if you're training for a race that'll take you longer than about 90 minutes to complete—you can run off your stores for anything shorter. Test gels, chews, and sports drinks on long, slow runs until you find something palatable that agrees with you.

4. **. . . AND THEN SIMULATE RACE-DAY STOMACH.** Start by eating your race-morning breakfast, and time it as you will on race day. Then do a long run that includes miles at or near race pace.

5. **IRON OUT KINKS.** If your go-to midrun fuel source sits like a rock in your stomach when you speed up, it's time to troubleshoot: No matter how many calories you take in midrun, they won't help if you're not digesting them. Try alternating between taking in carbs and taking sips of water—hydration promotes absorption. Slowing your intake can also help, so chase a small sip of gel with a small sip of water every few minutes instead of downing a whole gel at once. If it's still not working, it's back to the drawing board: Experiment with other fuels that might work better.

6. **PRACTICE, PRACTICE, PRACTICE.** The more you rehearse

your fueling (what, when, and how much you'll take in), the more likely your stomach will be to cooperate on race day. If you can schedule a tune-up race or two where you can practice in an adrenaline-rich environment, even better.

HOW TO PREVENT 4 COMMON GASTROINTESTINAL PROBLEMS[32]

However much you love running, it may not always agree with you. This is partially because the activity diverts blood flow away from your guts and toward working muscles, and partially because the up-and-down motion of running jostles around whatever may be in your stomach and intestines. About 60 percent of runners experience GI issues at some point. If you're among them, dietary changes can help. Here's what to do, depending on your symptoms.

1. **HEARTBURN.** People who regularly experience the burning associated with acid reflux—about 20 percent of adults—may find that it worsens during running. To lessen symptoms, steer clear of triggering foods like coffee and mints, prerun core work, and apparel that's too tight around the waist.

2. **BLOATING AND GAS.** Fibrous foods that cause gas, like beans and cruciferous vegetables, could be the culprit, so avoid them the night before or day of a run. Swallowing air can also make you gassy, so avoid chewing gum, and have a go-to calming routine to prevent nervous hyperventilating.

3. **NAUSEA.** Eating too much before or during a run can cause this, as can ingesting midrun fuel when you're not

> **BONUS TIP** If you're experiencing fever, chills, nausea, and diarrhea after you finish a run, you may be working too hard for your current fitness level. Back off and build up slowly for a few months, making sure to stay hydrated during and after runs.

used to it. Practice taking gels or chews in training to help your stomach accept them, and, when in doubt, take them more gradually, with sips of water between each slurp or bite.

4. **DIARRHEA.** Look at what you took in the previous day and that morning: Big meals, high-fiber foods, and sugary foods can all contribute to the poops. Some pain relievers like ibuprofen and naproxen can make gut inflammation worse, so avoid those, too.

---

6 CHANGES TO MAKE TO AVOID BARFING POSTRUN[33]

While nobody *enjoys* puking, some runners think doing it after a hard workout or race is proof that you really gave your all. Those runners are almost always wrong. Sprinting then spewing is usually caused at least in part by your food and drink choices. If you make these changes and you *still* hurl, congrats—you really did push until you puked.

1. **EAT, THEN WAIT.** Heavy breathing can create pressure in your abdominal cavity. If your stomach is fairly full prerun, that's a recipe for disaster. Try having your prerun meal or snack further in advance—2 to 3 hours is usually safe.

2. **PRACTICE FUELING SLOWLY.** When you run, your body diverts blood away from your digestive system and toward working muscles. This effect increases as you run harder, and it's more pronounced in the heat. If you eat or drink too much before, during, or after a hard effort, you'll boot. When you're going long enough to need midrun fuel, take in a small sip of sports drink or gel followed by a small sip of water, wait, and repeat.

3. **HYDRATE WELL.** Dehydration also slows digestion, so taking sips of water throughout a hard effort reduces your nausea risk.

4. **AVOID PUKE-INDUCING FOODS.** Anything acidic, such as citrus fruits or juices, as well as anything high in fat, fiber, or protein, can slow digestion. Stick to mostly bland, simple carbs prerun.

5. **MEDICATE.** An hour before a hard run, taking antacids or Pepto-Bismol might tamp down the urge to purge.

6. **KEEP MOVING.** Slowing to a walk or stopping entirely after running really hard can startle your stomach into spewing. Instead, keep jogging to ease your tummy's return to rest.

---

5 WAYS TO LIMIT DISASTROUS RESULTS IF YOU *MUST* ATTEMPT A BEER MILE[34]

It sounds like some kind of hazing ritual: Chug a beer, run a lap of a track, and repeat three more times. Yet some runners find the beer mile an intriguing challenge. Drinking four beers so quickly is considered binge drinking, so it isn't healthy. But if you're set on trying it, here's how to make it less bad for you (and others).

1. **FIND A DESIGNATED DRIVER!!!** It's so important that it's worth shouting. Do not drive after beer mile-ing. End of story.

2. **TIME IT RIGHT.** Don't attempt a beer mile if you're sick or sleep-deprived, or if you've had more than a single drink in the 4 to 6 hours leading up to the race.

3. **CAFFEINATE.** Having some coffee or a caffeinated gel about 45 minutes before

starting might prevent a severe dip in your energy levels midrace.

4. **EAT A LITTLE SOMETHING.** A bland snack like saltines 15 minutes prior to go time may slow your body's absorption of alcohol.

5. **DON'T MAKE PLANS.** You'll need about 5 hours to metabolize the alcohol you take in during a beer mile. Eat, hydrate, and prepare for a hangover.

TEN

EVERYDAY EATING

4 REASONS TO EAT A PROTEIN-PACKED BREAKFAST[1]

Protein: It's not just for gym rats looking to make "gainz." (And it's much tastier when you steer clear of protein powders and eat real food.) The nutrient helps repair muscle damage from any type of activity—running included—but that's not all.

1. **IT KEEPS YOU FULL.** Take in at least 30 grams of protein at breakfast and you'll delay the release of ghrelin, a hormone that makes you feel hungry, and increase the release of satiety hormones.

2. **IT HELPS YOU LOSE.** Research suggests that the aforementioned feeling of satiety can contribute to weight loss. If you're already at your goal weight, know that regularly eating a healthy breakfast can help you stay there.

3. **IT PREVENTS A CRASH.** A breakfast that's almost entirely refined carbs taxes your pancreas and causes blood sugar spikes. Protein won't do you like that.

4. **IT POWERS YOUR RUN.** Have some protein before a morning workout and you'll avoid tapping into the stores you need to

recover well. This is especially important when you'll be running for an hour or longer.

4 REASONS TO TAKE IT EASY ON THE COFFEE[2]

We were going to include a detailed list of coffee's many benefits—it's antioxidant-rich! It lowers your risk of diabetes and heart disease! It makes you feel awesome!—but then we realized that most of us don't need an excuse to drink *more*. You reap all the benefits of coffee after just a cup or two per day—here's what chugging it from dawn 'til dusk can do to you.

1. **IT MAY AFFECT PREGNANCY.** Research shows a link between high coffee consumption and miscarriage. While the two may simply be correlated, most doctors recommend pregnant women avoid exceeding 200 milligrams of caffeine per day—that's about one to two small cups.

2. **IT WEAKENS YOUR BONES.** Guzzling more than four cups daily may lower bone-mineral content, leaving you more prone to injuries like stress reactions and fractures.

3. **IT MESSES UP YOUR SLEEP.** Each person processes caffeine differently, but on average, it boosts alertness for 6 to 7 hours. Drinking coffee in the afternoon or evening can make it harder to doze off—meaning you'll need even *more* the next day.

4. **IT MAKES YOU FEEL CRAZY.** The jitters are real, and the more caffeine you take in, the more likely you are to feel alert in a neg-

ative way—jumpy, sweaty, and anxious. This effect can be more pronounced in already high-stress situations like before a race.

15 GREAT ANYTIME SNACKS FOR PEOPLE WHO GIVE A HOOT ABOUT HEALTH[3]

We've covered prerun, midrun, and postrun snacks, but what about the rest of the time, when you're not even thinking about running? Here's a list of quick options that are good for you even if you're *not* a runner. Have one of these on hand at all times so you never have to hit up a vending machine or snack bar.

1. High-fiber, low-sugar cereal with milk
2. Cottage cheese with fresh fruit
3. Plain yogurt with fresh fruit
4. Plain oatmeal with fresh fruit
5. Fresh-fruit smoothies made with plain yogurt or milk
6. Dried apricots or plums
7. Edamame
8. A banana, apple, or other porta-fruit
9. Carrots
10. Hummus with raw veggies and/or whole wheat crackers
11. Rice cakes with nut butter
12. String cheese
13. Tuna fish
14. Popcorn (lightly salted or seasoned with herbs)
15. Hard-boiled eggs

9 FOODS AND DRINKS RUNNERS SHOULD LIMIT (OR AVOID ENTIRELY)[4]

If most of your meals don't come from a drive-thru and a vegetable occasionally graces your plate, you're doing well compared to a lot of Americans. Still, that's not a high bar to clear, and you probably aren't willing to settle for being only slightly superior to your non-running peers. So put these items on your dietary high-alert list.

1. **FLAVORED YOGURTS.** There's a ton of sweetener—whether real sugar or the artificial stuff—in these, and it's best to avoid firing up your sweet tooth unless you need quick calories before or during a run. Instead, try plain Greek yogurt, which is especially rich in protein, and top it with fruit and nuts.

2. **MULTIGRAIN BREAD.** The word "multigrain" alone doesn't mean much, since breads labeled this way may still be made of refined flours and loaded with added sugar. When in doubt, check the ingredients list. Whole wheat or another whole grain flour should be first, and you shouldn't see the words "enriched" or "bleached."

3. **SPORTS DRINKS.** Save these for during or after very hot runs and runs that last at least an hour.

4. **ANYTHING "PARTIALLY HYDROGENATED."** If you see these words on a label, put that product back on the shelf. Oil that's been processed in that way has trans fat, which increases your cholesterol levels. Companies aren't required to list trans fat in the nutrition facts if there's less than half a gram per serving.

5. **BEER.** Be especially wary of beer after a run or race: Stick to just one, because the alcohol dehydrates you further, and alternate sips of beer with sips of water.

6. **ENERGY DRINKS.** They give you wings—and lots and lots of sweetener. Plus, a 2014 study found that athletes who slurped energy drinks experienced negative effects like nervousness and insomnia that lasted after their competition. Caffeine is the performance enhancer in these products, so get it from coffee or an energy gel instead.

7. **YOUR BELOVED NUTELLA (AND PRODUCTS LIKE IT).** Nut butters are great for you, when they're made of just nuts and

salt. Check the label and avoid anything that has more than a few grams of sugar per serving, and again, anything with hydrogenated oils.

8. **PROTEIN PRODUCTS.** Bars and shakes should never be an everyday thing. Even if you're trying to bulk up, you're better off getting protein from real food sources like eggs, poultry, fish, legumes, and dairy.

9. **SODA.** Duh, right? But if you just love that fizzy sweetness, and you think the no-calorie diet variety is acceptable, think again. Artificial sweeteners may mess with your beneficial gut bacteria and raise your risk of developing diabetes, per a 2014 study. Most days, drink just plain old water. Flavor it with lemon or lime juice if you're feeling fancy.

3 WAYS TO CURB YOUR ADDED-SUGAR INTAKE[5]

Even if you've sworn off soda, candy, and caffeinated drinks that are more syrup than coffee, you're probably still eating a boatload of added sugar. It lurks in unexpected places—yogurt! salad dressings! bread!—and it can cause chronic disease, extra fat, and a ravenous appetite. The FDA recommends getting no more than 10 percent of your daily calories from added sugar—that's about 50 grams. What's confusing is that naturally occurring sugar, like in produce and dairy, is A-OK, because those foods are packed with vitamins, minerals, and fiber. Here's how to tell the difference between the good and the bad stuff.

1. **CHECK THE LABEL.** If any of these terms are among the first five items on the ingredients list, put down that product: sucrose, brown sugar, corn syrup, dextrose, fructose, high-fructose corn syrup, honey, maple syrup, or raw cane syrup/sugar. (The obvious exception is when you're looking for gels, chews, or other on-the-run fuel.)

2. **COMPARE.** To distinguish added sugars from naturally

occurring ones, compare a plain product to its sweetened counterpart. For example, if a 6-ounce container of strawberry yogurt has 18 grams of sugar, and a plain yogurt of the same size has 9, you'll know the flavored one has 9 grams of added sugar.

> **BONUS TIP** Artificial sweeteners don't activate the brain's reward centers like real sugar does, which may lead to a future real-sugar binge.[6] Instead of turning to the fake stuff, gradually cut down on the amount of sugary foods and drinks you consume: The less you have, the less you'll crave.[7]

3. **CHECK THE LABEL.** An "added sugars" line is coming to all nutrition labels in July 2018, which will eliminate any guesswork. Thanks, FDA![8]

5 GOOD SOURCES OF COMPLETE PROTEIN[9]

As a runner, you need .54 to .91 grams of protein per pound of body weight daily—the lower end on easy-run days, an in-between amount on tougher days, and the higher end if you're running hard *and* pumping iron. Take in too little and your muscles won't recover properly from your workouts—which means fatigue at best, and a sidelining injury at worst. These foods have all nine of the amino acids that muscles crave.

1. **CHIA SEEDS.** Mix 'em into oatmeal or yogurt to net 3 grams of protein per tablespoon.
2. **FISH.** Cod, for example, has 19 grams of protein (and just 89 calories) in a 3-ounce serving.
3. **GREEK YOGURT.** Six ounces have 17 grams of protein. Stick to plain and mix in fruit to avoid added sugar.
4. **MEAT.** When possible, choose lean meats like bison, white meat poultry, and lean beef. You'll get 24 grams of protein from 3 ounces of sirloin tip side steak.
5. **SOYBEANS.** A half cup of shelled edamame offers 9 grams

of protein. Tofu and other soy products are also good options.

---

7 THINGS TO KNOW IF YOU WANT TO STOP EATING ANIMALS[10]

First of all: You *can* stop eating meat (and fish, and dairy, and all other animal products) and still be a successful athlete. A handful of pros, including recently retired ultrarunner Scott Jurek, are entirely plant-powered. However, do it wrong and your energy levels and overall health will suffer. Here's some basic know-how.

1. **MAKE A PROTEIN PLAN.** You need protein to keep your muscles and immune system strong. Eggs and dairy are a good source if you're not going full vegan. If you are, try lentils, nuts, beans, tofu, seeds, soy milk, almond milk, or grains like quinoa, bulgur, and oats.

2. **TAKE IN MORE IRON AND ZINC.** Your body doesn't absorb plant-based sources of these nutrients—which play a role in how well your body functions while running—as well as animal-based sources. So load up on iron-rich (spinach, soybeans, lentils, quinoa, and beans) and zinc-rich (grains, legumes, nuts, and soy products) foods, and get enough vitamin C from leafy greens and citrus fruits to promote absorption.

3. **FORTIFY YOUR DIET.** Vitamin B_{12}, which is needed to prevent anemia, primarily exists in animal-based sources. If you're still eating dairy products and eggs, you can get it from there; if not, you may need to choose B_{12}-fortified products.

4. **ADD HEALTHY FATS.** If you're not eating fish, you're missing out on a big source of omega-3 fatty acids, which reduce inflammation and support brain function. Walnuts, flaxseed, avocado, pumpkin seeds, and soybeans are vegan sources of omega-3s.

5. **EASE IN.** Once you understand the principles of a healthy vegetarian or vegan diet, start by removing one animal-based food

per week and replacing it with a protein-rich alternative. For example, if you typically eat scrambled eggs for breakfast, do a tofu scramble instead.

6. **WATCH THE SCALE.** If you're losing too much weight or generally feeling fatigued, that's a sign that you're not getting enough calories. Try increasing your healthy-fat intake: Sauté veggies in olive oil, spread avocado on your sandwiches, or snack on nuts and seeds.

7. **WHEN IN DOUBT, SEE A DIETITIAN.** If you cut out meat or other animal-based products and aren't feeling like yourself, call in help. An expert can identify tweaks you can make to ensure your energy levels stay high and your body stays healthy and nourished.

7 OCCASIONS THAT CALL FOR
A NIGHTTIME SNACK[11]

That advice you may have heard about not eating after a certain time at night? Yeah, that's not always wise. Hunger makes it hard to fall or stay asleep (as any marathoner who's zombie-walked to the fridge during training can attest), and you need sleep to recover properly and perform your best. Here are the perfect snacks for any situation.

1. **IF YOUR SWEET TOOTH IS ACHING, HAVE:** a blend of frozen blueberries and watermelon. You'll get plenty of natural sugars and antioxidants without a ton of calories.

2. **IF YOUR WORKOUT WAS HARD, LONG, OR BOTH, HAVE:** a small glass of chocolate milk. Consuming one protein, casein, found in milk helps muscles repair overnight, and the sugar helps restock your glycogen stores.

3. **IF YOUR GOAL IS TO LOSE WEIGHT (BUT YOU'RE FAMISHED), HAVE:** plain Greek yogurt with cinnamon and vanilla extract. A 2014 study suggests having this snack 30 minutes before bed can increase your metabolism the next day.

4. **IF PRERACE ANXIETY IS MAKING SLEEPING TOUGH, HAVE:** a few crackers with an ounce of cheddar or Swiss cheese. The tryptophan and refined carbs in this combo promote snooziness.

5. **IF YOU'RE BASICALLY AN INSOMNIAC, HAVE:** 8 ounces of tart cherry juice, twice a day (including one dose shortly before bed) for 2 weeks. Its naturally occurring melatonin can regulate out-of-whack sleep cycles.

6. **IF YOU'VE GOT AN EARLY, PRE-BREAKFAST RUN PLANNED, HAVE:** a piece of whole grain toast topped with strawberries and nut butter, 3 hours after dinner. The complex carbs and protein may tide you over through the next morning.

7. **IF YOU RAN WITHIN A FEW HOURS OF BEDTIME, HAVE:** a whole wheat tortilla filled with scrambled eggs and vegetables. The protein in the eggs prevents the midnight wake-up, and the veggies are just good for you.

ELEVEN

IN THE KITCHEN

---

5 WAYS TO ENJOY COOKING (ALMOST) AS MUCH AS YOU ENJOY RUNNING

No matter what you order when you go out to eat, it almost certainly has more salt, fat, and/or sugar than a dish you would prepare yourself. (That's why restaurant meals taste so good!) But one study found that dining out twice per week or more resulted in an average weight gain of a quarter pound per year,[1] which can add up—and slow you down. Follow these guidelines and you might actually *enjoy* prepping your own grub.

1. **HAVE A GOOD PLAN.** A recipe is like a training plan. If you follow one, you're more likely to get the desired results. You'd trust a plan from a well-known coach more than one you found on some random blog, and the same goes for recipes: Those from cookbooks, magazines, and well-known food sites are most likely to actually work.
2. **AND KNOW THE PLAN.** Just as you'd read a training plan all the way through before committing, you need to carefully size up a recipe. You don't want to buy all the ingredients only to discover that you need a gadget you don't have.

3. **KEEP IT SIMPLE.** You wouldn't tell a new runner to cover 20 miles, would you? If you're a kitchen noob, start with recipes that require fewer ingredients and less prep time.

4. **JUST BUY THE SPICES. SERIOUSLY.** If a recipe demands a trip to the spice aisle for things you don't already have, just get them— even if you're outraged that a tiny canister costs $5 and you'll only need a little bit for this particular recipe. Spices are the difference between a "meh" meal and a marvelous one. Keep cooking, and you'll eventually use the rest.

5. **FUEL UP.** Running and cooking are both activities that are nearly impossible to do when your stomach is growling. Instead of caving to the desire to order a pizza, have a small "chef's snack"—a handful of nuts, a couple cubes of cheese, or some chips and salsa—to take the edge off.

10 MEAL-PREP TIPS FOR BUSY, HEALTH-CONSCIOUS RUNNERS[2]

The thing about healthy, whole foods is that they take longer to prepare than the processed crap you can unwrap and eat. If you're accustomed to waiting until you're hungry to grab something, you're likely grabbing garbage. Or if you wait until you're hungry to buy a healthy meal, you're likely going broke. Avoid these fates by meal preppin'—it's easy.

1. **SET ASIDE A FEW HOURS ON A SUNDAY.** This assumes you work Monday through Friday—if not, choose the day before your workweek begins.

2. **BEGIN WITH LUNCHES.** This is the meal you're most likely to want to be able to grab, fully prepared, as you rush out the door. You can make a healthy breakfast quickly, and you may be less rushed in the evening as you cook dinner.

3. **CHOOSE REUSABLE.** Sure, snack and sandwich baggies are convenient, but they're also wasteful. Opt for plastic or glass containers you can use again and again.

4. **KEEP IT SIMPLE.** Now's not the time for complex recipes.

5. **START WITH PROTEIN . . .** You can do a lot as you roast a whole chicken or bake a whole mess of salmon. Preheat the oven, season your protein of choice, and pop it in.

6. **. . . AND CARBS.** Quinoa, whole grain rice, or lentils plus lean meat plus veggies equals a healthy, satisfying meal. Get a big batch going at the start of your meal-prep session.

7. **CHOP, CHOP.** Cut fresh veggies into bite-size pieces for snacking, roasting, or salad topping.

8. **CONSIDER SOUPS AND SALADS . . .** A giant pot of soup will easily last you the whole week (possibly longer, if you freeze some), and you can throw your protein and chopped veggies on a salad.

9. **. . . AND ROASTED-VEGGIE SIDES.** Toss chopped veggies with olive oil, salt, and pepper, spread them on a baking sheet, and stick them in the oven while your protein is cooking.

10. **PORTION EVERYTHING OUT.** You'll want one lunch main course with protein, carbs, and healthy fats per day, plus a morning and afternoon snack. For afternoon snacks, put raw veggies into five small containers with a blob of hummus or nut butter for dipping. A piece of fruit with a string cheese or a handful of nuts makes a great morning snack.

3 ITEMS TO PURGE FROM YOUR KITCHEN[3]

You want the stuff you prepare and consume in this room to make you a better runner, not a slower (or sicker) one. Toss this stuff to ensure that happens.

1. **EXPIRED FOOD.** Go through your fridge at least monthly (and your pantry yearly) to filter out things that are past their prime *before* they end up in your belly. If you find yourself wasting a lot of fresh fruits and veggies, consider buying a smaller amount of fresh stuff and a greater amount of frozen the next time you're at the store—most produce won't last 7-plus days, which can be a problem if you shop weekly.

2. **HUGE PLATES OR BOWLS.** If you have a larger plate to fill, you're likely to fill it—and not always with the healthy stuff that should be taking up the most real estate. Plus, being able to stuff very small bowls with treats like ice cream can help the snack feel more satisfying.

3. **FOODS YOU CAN'T STOP EATING.** Everyone has a binge trigger, whether it's cookies, potato chips, or even sweetened breakfast cereal. Your best bet is to throw out what you have and avoid buying any more.

TWELVE

WEIGHT LOSS AND MAINTENANCE

2 VARIABLES TO TRACK FOR WEIGHT LOSS OR MAINTENANCE[1]

Many runners know that while logging miles burns a lot of calories, it's entirely possible to eat enough that you *gain* weight—even while marathon training. (Oh, cruel world!) Luckily, it's simple (if not easy) to avoid that fate.

1. **LOG YOUR FOOD AND DRINK INTAKE.** All the time is best, but even a monthlong log can help you identify times when you tend to overdo it and the foods that are especially dangerous for you. Awareness is the first step toward breaking the habit of a post-long-run pint (of beer or of ice cream).

2. **TRACK YOUR WEIGHT.** Research shows that weight-losers who hop on the scale daily are more likely to keep it off than those who check in less frequently. Expect some fluctuations from day to day, but when the scale has trended up for more than a few days, that's a red flag.

7 BEHAVIORS THAT HELP YOU LOSE OR MAINTAIN WEIGHT . . . [2]

If you're already running, congrats—you've stumbled upon one key behavior that'll help you slim down (or stay slim). To complement your current efforts, try a few of these tactics.

1. **RUN JUST A BIT MORE.** Tack on 10 to 15 minutes to any given run and you'll burn that many more calories. Get up just a little earlier to squeeze in the extra mile or so.

2. **ENJOY YOURSELF.** Research suggests that you're more likely to make healthy food choices after a workout when you've had fun doing it. So find a way to have fun midrun, by meeting up with a group, streaming a sitcom from your treadmill, or whatever floats your boat.

3. **REFUEL WITH CARE.** Unless you've just finished a hard or long run, a glass of water (and maybe a piece of fruit) should be enough on the refueling front. Overrewarding yourself is one way to erase the weight-loss benefits of a workout.

4. **BUY SMALLER DISHES.** Cornell University research has found that most adults eat 92 percent of what's on their plates at meals. Smaller plates and bowls may help you feel just as satisfied with a smaller portion.[3]

5. **HIT THE GYM.** The age-related decline of muscle mass is one reason your metabolism slows as you get older. Running builds up your lower body, but targeted strength training can stop losses elsewhere *and* can complement running's effect on your quads, hamstrings, calves, and glutes.

6. **TRACK YOUR ACTIVITY.** Wearable tech that counts steps and calorie burn may motivate you to move more. The more you move, the more likely you are to shed pounds and keep them off.

7. **CONNECT WITH A HEALTHY CREW.** Obesity is socially contagious, per research—but so are healthy habits. Surround

yourself, whether in real life, on social media, or both, with folks who share your desire to be fit and healthy, and you'll be better equipped to achieve your goals.

. . . AND 8 COMMON WEIGHT-LOSS MISTAKES TO AVOID[4]

It can take a lot of work to see a lower number on the scale. And if you're misdirecting your energy, you'll be toiling hard only to see the same reading, day after day, or worse—a higher one. Don't waste your efforts and make sure you're not making these errors.

1. **MISCOUNTING CALORIES.** It's easy to overestimate how many you're burning and underestimate how many you're taking in. Luckily, there are apps that help you keep an accurate count. They'll use variables like your height, weight, and sex to determine what you burn during activity, and you can log specific food and drink information after every meal or snack.

2. **GOING LOW-FAT.** The era of fat as public enemy #1 has come and gone. Today we know that fat is crucial for health (it helps your body absorb key vitamins) and for feeling sated (so you don't gorge on junk). Prioritize the unsaturated variety found in avocados, nuts, seeds, fish, and olive oil.

3. **FASTING BEFORE RUNNING.** While it's true that your body will eventually burn fat on a fasted run, because it takes more energy to turn fat into fuel, it prefers to use your muscles' glycogen stores first. Once the glycogen stores are sapped, you hit the wall: You'll be forced to slow down, *and* you'll likely be cranky and miserable. You don't need to eat before you run if you're going short and easy, but otherwise, fuel up—you'll have a better-quality workout and burn more calories.

4. **FASTING AFTER RUNNING.** You need to have a snack with protein and carbs within an hour of harder or longer workouts. Why? Skip it, and runger (that is, postrun hunger) will hit you like a truck in a few hours—not the best way to prevent a binge.

5. **OVERFUELING MIDRUN.** If you just can't get enough of sugary gels or sports drinks, listen up: You don't need them on runs that are shorter than 60 to 75 minutes. If you're going longer, you should take in 30 to 60 grams of carbs per hour from your source of choice.

6. **OVERLOOKING WHAT YOU DRINK.** Research shows something you likely already know: Calorie-laden liquids don't make you feel full. Therefore, whatever calories you drink will simply pile up atop your daily food intake. Stick with calorie-free bevvies as much as possible. And limit alcohol consumption: It packs the double whammy of extra calories *and* lowered inhibition surrounding overeating.

7. **CRASH DIETING.** Life isn't *The Biggest Loser*. Sustainable weight loss takes time. Instead of overhauling your diet, drastically cutting calories, and doubling up on workouts all at once, make one small change at a time: Cut out soda one week. Drop your postdinner bowl of ice cream the next. You're more likely to keep off pounds you lose slowly, say 1 or 2 per week, than those you drop via changes you can't keep up long-term.

8. **NOT ACCOUNTING FOR PROGRESS.** The sad reality is, the less you weigh, the fewer calories you need, and the fewer calories you burn during activity. If you're using an app, keep your weight up to date. If you're not, scale down your calorie intake after losing 10 to 15 percent of your starting weight.

---

6 BAD DIET HABITS (AND HOW TO BREAK THEM)[5]

You've probably heard the phrase "you can't outrun a bad diet." It's the truth: It's a helluva lot easier to inhale a huge number of empty calories than it is to run long or hard enough to burn said calories off. And even if you buy into the wisdom of this oft-repeated nugget, you may still be making one (or more) of these mistakes.

1. **EVENING BINGES.** This is when you're most likely to be home, with time and access to all your favorite eats. If you've been putting off snacks and meals all day due to other obligations, you're probably starving. Bring healthy, portable options with you to work and have dinner ASAP upon returning home—it's too easy for a predinner snack to turn into an all-evening graze.

2. **RELYING ON ENERGY BARS.** These are high in calories (they can have 300 or more) and are not meant for everyday consumption. Use them only when you're fueling up for a hard or long workout, or when you aren't able to eat a legit meal. (Even then, whole foods like a piece of fruit and some almonds would be better.)

3. **EATING TOO MANY CARBS.** Sure, runners love pasta, and bagels, and crusty Italian bread, but every bite of those foods takes up stomach space that could go to more nutritious and less caloric foods such as fruits, veggies, and beans. Fill at least half your plate at every meal with produce, and eat that half before you touch your precious carbs.

4. **EATING TOO MUCH, GENERALLY.** After a long run, or at the end of a high-volume training week, your inner monologue

might be saying, "Feed me! Feed me!" on repeat. That's fair, but if you try to quiet the voice with a massive meal, you risk storing most of the calories as fat. Instead, have a small meal—one that leaves you just satisfied, not stuffed—and if you're hungry in a couple hours, have another.

5. **CELEBRATING EVERY RUN WITH FOOD.** Research shows that, if you look back on an exercise session as hard, you're more likely to pig out postrun. Save that instinct, and instead, have a normal meal after workouts and reserve the celebratory meal for after a race—it'll feel much more special if it's truly out of the ordinary.

6. **CELEBRATING EVERY RUN WITH DRINKS.** Alcohol has a lot of calories and not much nutritional punch. So if your buddies like to go out to boozy brunch after every long run, change your routine. Save the postrun imbibing for once or twice a month, max, and suggest a postrun coffee instead. Bonus: It's cheaper!

---

4 SURPRISING CAUSES OF WEIGHT GAIN[6]

If you're up a few pounds after, say, a weeklong vacation, you might be disappointed but not shocked—and it's easy to return to baseline at home, where ice cream is no longer considered an acceptable meal. But if your weight's creeping up despite your best intentions, see if any of these sneaky culprits might be to blame.

1. **A MESSY KITCHEN.** One Cornell study found that subjects who had access to cookies in a kitchen with a sink full of dirty dishes ate twice as many cookies as subjects in a clean kitchen. Another found a correlation between a higher weight and leaving snacks out on the countertop. Consider your kitchen a sacred space: Keep it tidy, and if you *must* buy stuff that tempts you to binge, hide it. Store fruit in a bowl on your counter and you'll be more likely to choose it over less nutritious options.

2. **MISLEADING LABELS.** Research shows that words like

"natural," "healthy," and even "organic" on food labels promote greater consumption. The healthiest foods don't come in packages that tout their health benefits. If you are shopping for a packaged food, ignore the marketing hype and go straight to its nutrition label. People who read them tend to weigh less than those who don't.

3. **PAYING WITH PLASTIC.** You're more likely to make impulse purchases if you're using a credit card. Instead, make a list in advance, stick to it, and pay with cash. If you must make a checkout-line impulse purchase, make it a calorie-free magazine—may we suggest *Runner's World*?

4. **DISTRACTED EATING.** Anything you can do to eat more slowly and savor your food more will produce better weight-loss results—you're less likely to notice that you've eaten enough to feel satisfied if you're shoveling in a meal while reading or watching TV.

3 CLUES THAT A TRENDY DIET IS BULLSHIT

Paleo! Gluten-free! Atkins! Whatever the latest popular word or phrase that precedes "diet" is when you're reading this book! The lure of a miracle diet can be tempting to type-A runners, whether they're seeking weight loss, improved performance, or both. But if a diet requires any of these sacrifices, don't believe the hype.

1. **IT SEVERELY LIMITS HOW MANY CARBOHYDRATES YOU CAN EAT (INCLUDING BEFORE, DURING, AND AFTER WORKOUTS).** While there is some research to support a low-carb, high-fat diet for ultrarunners—who are running so long (and so slowly) that it may be advantageous for their bodies to learn to burn fat for fuel[7]—it's not practical for most of us. Why? For one, your body and brain are used to running on carbs,[8] and when you're low on them, you'll be miserable—especially during and after workouts. (The phenomenon known as "bonking" or "hitting the wall" happens when your

reserves are depleted.)[9] Plus, research shows that carbs are the best fuel for fast running,[10] so if you're trying to nail a time goal at any distance, carbs should fuel the workouts that get you there.

2. **IT SAYS YOU CAN NEVER, EVER HAVE A CERTAIN FOOD (OR FOODS).** Banning a food is the best way to ensure you crave that food more than ever.[11] It's better to try to eat well 80 to 90 percent of the time and allow yourself small indulgences the rest of the time.[12]

3. **IT PLACES SEVERE RESTRICTIONS ON ANY TYPE OF WHOLE FOOD.** For example, the low-carb, high-fat diet recommends you get just 5 percent of your carbohydrates from fruits and starches.[13] But you're most likely to get the vitamins and nutrients you need by eating a variety of brightly colored produce, *including* fruit.[14] Most runners should eat a mix of carbs, lean protein, and healthy fats and should consume most of their carbs in the form of fruits, vegetables, legumes, and whole grains.[15]

---

4 FOODS AND DRINKS THAT'LL HELP YOU SHED POUNDS[16]

The word "diet" is basically synonymous with "deprivation" and "despair," but it doesn't have to be: *Adding* certain foods and drinks to your regular rotation can help you reach your ideal weight. Try these.

1. **HIGH-FIBER WHOLE FOODS.** Each day, strive for at least three cups of veggies, three servings of fruit, and a few helpings of beans, whole grains, and fiber-rich starches. Fiber takes up some serious stomach space, promoting feelings of satiety, and the soluble kind (in beans and fruit) helps keep blood-sugar levels stable.

2. **BUGGY FOODS.** We're talking microscopic bugs: the bacteria that live in your gut and affect digestion. Certain strains can

promote weight loss, per research, so eat cultured dairy (kefir, yogurt) or other probiotic foods (tempeh, kimchi, sauerkraut) daily.

3. **SPICY STUFF.** Capsaicin—the compound that makes peppers hot—burns more than just your mouth: It may torch calories and help suppress appetite. Add red pepper flakes to soups and sauces to spice-ify more meals.

4. **GREEN TEA.** It has a class of polyphenols called catechins, which may promote calorie burning and keep hunger at bay. Try it instead of coffee for a less intense midday pick-me-up.

---

9 WAYS TO AVOID HOLIDAY WEIGHT GAIN

You may not be logging a ton of miles in November and December, but 'tis the season for overindulging with family, friends, and coworkers. It's common to put on some hibernation weight as days get shorter and temps drop, but if you're not interested in debating whether to unbutton your jeans after every meal or to invest in a pair of "fat pants," try these tactics.

1. **HAVE A PRE-PARTY SNACK.** Something full of fiber and lean protein—a small salad topped with a few pieces of grilled chicken, for example—will take the edge off your hunger and give you some nutrients not found in, say, pigs in a blanket. Limit it to 250 or fewer calories so you can have some hors d'oeuvres.

2. **BEWARE THE OFFICE FREE TABLE.** Keep healthy snacks on hand at work. If you're tempted to feast on the cookies a coworker brought in, remember your better option. A single indulgence won't hurt, but if midday desserts are a daily occurrence, you'll pack on pounds.

3. **TREAT YO'SELF POSTRUN . . .** A small slice of pumpkin pie (which has vitamin A!) after a long run will help you refuel and satisfy your sweet tooth. Your appetite may be suppressed

right after exercise, so you're unlikely to get creative with the definition of "small slice."

4. **. . . BUT DON'T OVERDO IT.** If it's possible to gain weight while marathon training—and it is!—it's certainly possible to gain weight while running primarily to burn calories in the off-season. Stick to healthy options most days.

5. **PARTITION YOUR PLATE.** At a holiday meal, fill about half your plate with veggies. Then split the other half between meat and starchy foods like sweet potatoes or stuffing.

6. **HYDRATE.** It's easy to forget to drink in cool weather and also to mistake thirst for hunger. Start every big meal or party with a glass of water.

7. **LIMIT THE BOOZE.** Beer, wine, and mixed drinks aren't just empty calories: Alcohol limits inhibition, which might make you say, "Screw it! I'll have as many cookies as I damn well please." Stick to no more than one or two drinks per day, and have a glass of water after each.

8. **MAKE SMART SWAPS.** Sweet wine is more caloric than light beer. Pecan pie (at about 500 calories per slice) is more caloric than just about any other dessert. Indulge in your most favorite things, but if you can take or leave something, leave it.

9. **BYO HEALTHY STUFF.** Most party or dinner hosts encourage contributions, so make yours nutrient dense. Bring a veggies-and-hummus tray to a party or a roasted-veggie side dish to a meal.

SECTION 3

126 GEAR TIPS

THE 4 GOLDEN RULES OF GEAR

---

1. **FIND YOUR PERFECT PAIR OF SHOES . . .** Running in uncomfortable shoes can lead to injury—and it also feels pretty crummy. A model that works for your friend or coworker won't necessarily work for you, which is why it's *so important* to go to a specialty store to get fitted. Do it at the end of the day when your feet are at their largest, bring the socks you'll train in, and make sure the store lets you run a little bit in the shoes before you buy them. You'll likely need a larger size than you do in street shoes to give your toes ample room as you run.[1]

2. **. . . OR PAIRS OF SHOES . . .** Research shows runners who have multiple shoe models in their rotation are 39 percent less likely to get injured than those who stick to one pair.[2] Try a well-cushioned pair (or two) for everyday and long runs and a lighter pair (or two) for speedwork and tempo runs.

3. **. . . AND REPLACE THEM REGULARLY.** The rule of thumb is to replace running shoes once they've covered 300 to 500 miles,[3] but if you're too lazy to keep track, tune in to how

you feel. If you notice more aches or fatigue than usual when you're running in a certain pair, it may be time to retire them.[4] (Worn-down treads are another clue.)

4. **AVOID OVERDRESSING.** Take the current temperature and dress as if it were 10 degrees warmer, except on cool, windy days.[5] If you still regularly find yourself uncomfortable midrun, let our What to Wear Tool (runnersworld.com/whattowear) be your guide.

---

11 WAYS TO SAVE MONEY ON GEAR[6, 7]

Cheapskates love running: The only real expense is a good pair of shoes. (Why *are* they so pricey, anyway?) Here's how to get those—and other stuff—on the cheap.

1. **GO ONLINE . . .** If you already know the shoe model and size that works for you, you may be able to find it at a deep discount online.

2. **. . . OR DON'T.** Expos and specialty-store sales offer discounted shoes and gear, too. Plus, you avoid shipping fees and the risk of having to pay to return the item if it doesn't fit right.

3. **KNOW THE SALES.** November, January, and June are when new models of shoes usually debut; that's when your local store will have old models on sale. Look for deeply discounted apparel in February and August, and on Black Friday.

4. **USE A CLUB DISCOUNT.** If you belong to your local running club, you may be eligible to save at local stores.

5. **ASK FOR A DISCOUNT.** See if your running store will match prices you've found online.

6. **WORK PART-TIME.** If you can snag a few shifts at your gym or specialty store, you may be eligible for discounts or freebies.

7. **BE LESS PICKY . . .** Strange colors and patterns in shoes and apparel often end up on the sale rack fastest.

8. **. . . OR BE MORE PICKY.** If you actually care about matching and/or not looking ridiculous on the run, you'll never wear the

cheap-but-loud tights or top. It's only a bargain if it's something you'll use.

9. **GUINEA-PIG YOUR FEET.** Major shoe companies send testers free shoes in exchange for feedback before they release new models. It helps if you're a sample size (a men's 9 or a women's 7) and you run at least 30 miles per week.

10. **BECOME AN AMBASSADOR.** If you have enough clout on social media, or a big enough blog following, a company may send you free shoes or apparel in exchange for publicity.

11. **RACE FASTER.** Many hometown events give gift certificates to local running stores as awards.

THIRTEEN

SHOES

THE BEST WAY TO TIE YOUR SHOES . . .[1]

If you double- (or triple- or quadruple-) knot your laces and they still come untied midrun, you might be ready to invest in shoes that fasten with Velcro. Instead, try the reef knot.

- Cross the left lace over the right lace, then pull it through.
- Make a loop (or "bunny ear") on the left, then bring the lace on the right side atop (so, closer to your ankle than to your toes) the loop.
- Continue the right lace around and feed it into the hole you just made.
- Grab both loops to pull the knot tight.

. . . AND 5 DIFFERENT WAYS TO LACE THEM TO CURE FOOT PAIN[2]

Sometimes, running in the wrong type of shoe for your body or gait is what causes foot pain. But if you've been fitted at a specialty store and you've still got pain, try lacing your shoes differently depending on where your feet hurt.

THE PAIN Friction in one spot atop your foot
THE FIX Lacing around the problem area
HOW TO Lace your shoes as normal, with your foot inside. When you reach the spot that usually bugs you, instead of lacing across it, pull the laces through the bottom of the next eyelet on that side to leave a gap on the tongue. Continue lacing as normal above the problem spot.

THE PAIN The entire top of your foot feels too much pressure
THE FIX Parallel lacing
HOW TO Lace the first two eyelets on your big-toe side from underneath. Bring the lace from the first eyelet

straight across and push it through the first eyelet on the opposite side. Pull it straight up the side, skipping one eyelet, and thread it through the third eyelet on the opposite side. Repeat until you reach the top, then do the same with the lace in the second eyelet.

THE PAIN Big-toe pain (and/or a black big toenail)
THE FIX Zigzag lacing to eliminate pressure from the upper
HOW TO Thread one end of the lace through the eyelet closest your big toe and pull that end under and through the eyelet closest to your ankle on the opposite side. Leave enough slack to tie a bow. Take the other end of the lace and pull it through the opposite eyelet, then diagonally across, under, and through until you reach the top.

THE PAIN All your toes feel cramped
THE FIX The double-shoelace method allows the top half of your foot to have a roomier fit
HOW TO Take out your laces, measure them, then buy two sets of laces half the length. Use one lace to go halfway up

your foot, bunny-knotting at the midfoot, then continuing with another lace to bunny-knot again at the top.

THE PAIN Sliding heel, shifting shoe
THE FIX Adding loops to the top of your laces to tighten the fit around the ankle
HOW TO Lace normally. Come up from under the second-to-last eyelet and send each lace straight up and down through the top eyelet on the same side to make a loop. Cross the laces through the opposite-side loops and tie as normal.

BONUS TIP[3] If the fit or feel of your shoes is just a bit off, try swapping out the sock liner. For example, if a shoe is just a hair too roomy, a thicker liner may help. Once you have new liners to try, remove the old ones and place them atop the new, lining them up at the heel. Trace around the old liner and cut off any excess to ensure the new one sits in the shoe properly.

4 STEPS TO TAKE TO DETERMINE YOUR ARCH HEIGHT[4]

Your arch height is one factor that determines which type of shoe you'll need. Here's how to know whether yours is low, normal, or high.

- Fill a shallow pan halfway with water.
- Step in it barefoot to wet your entire sole.

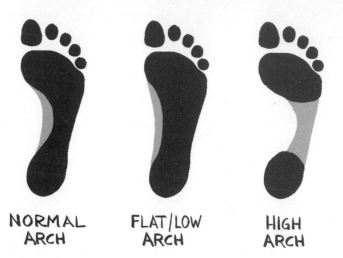

NORMAL ARCH   FLAT/LOW ARCH   HIGH ARCH

- Step onto a paper bag or other piece of heavy paper and shift your weight onto that leg.
- Remove your foot and compare its print with these drawings.

Normal (medium) arch. Congrats: You can wear just about any shoe! Your arch probably supports your body weight, and your feet likely pronate (that is, roll inward) a normal amount.

Flat (low) arch. You'll likely need a more supportive shoe to stop your foot from overpronating (rolling inward too much) as you run.

High arch. You're not likely to experience pronation problems, but because your arch is high, your feet don't absorb shock as well. Your best bet is probably a well-cushioned shoe.

> **BONUS TIP** Heavier shoes weigh you down: An additional 3.5 ounces of weight per shoe will cause you to slow by about 1 percent.[5] That said, the longer you're running, the more support and cushioning you'll need to stay comfortable. Choose lightweight shoes for speedwork and 5K and 10K races, midweight shoes for tempo runs and half marathons, and something more supportive for long runs and full marathons.

FOURTEEN

CLOTHING

---

5 STEPS TO LESS-STINKY TECH FABRIC[1]

1. **SHOWER, THEN STRIP.** This preliminary rinse will wash away at least some odor-causing bacteria before they proliferate.[2]
2. **GENTLY WRING AND AIR-DRY.** You don't want even slightly damp clothing to rot away in your hamper.
3. **TURN EVERYTHING INSIDE OUT.**
4. **WASH IN COLD WATER WITH A CUP OF VINEGAR AND LESS DETERGENT THAN USUAL.** And avoid fabric softeners at all costs—these products coat the tech fibers and prevent water and detergent from working their magic.
5. **DRY CLOTHES ON LOW HEAT.** High heat messes with the elastic. Air-dry if a piece's label tells you to.

---

3 ARGUMENTS FOR RUNNING IN COTTON . . .

1. **PEOPLE DID IT FOR YEARS.** The first running boom took place in the 1970s. Tech fabric wasn't developed until the mid-'90s.[3] Somehow, runners survived.

2. **EVERYONE ALREADY HAS IT.** Even beginners who haven't worked out since their last high-school phys-ed class likely already own some cotton tees. Having to buy new clothes is just one more excuse to put off getting started.

3. **IT STINKS LESS.** Research shows that odor-producing bacteria continue to multiply in tech fabrics long after a workout has ended,[4] and putting tech gear through the wash isn't always enough to fully de-stink it.[5]

. . . AND 2 ARGUMENTS AGAINST IT

1. **BLISTERS.** If you're venturing into the world of tech gear, buy socks first.[6] Cotton absorbs sweat, which creates friction, and because shoes block airflow and prevent evaporation, your feet will likely be the first casualties of an all-cotton wardrobe.

2. **CHAFING.** Again, because of cotton's sponge-like properties, any hot spots like your nipples, inner thighs, and pits will become infinitely more irritable in cotton than in tech fabric. And forget running in extreme heat (with extreme sweat) or rain.

> **BONUS TIP** If you lack the pockets to store midrun fuel, grab some safety pins. If you use gels, pin the part you'd pull off to the outside of your waistband and allow the rest of the gel to flop to the inside, against your skin. When you're ready to take it, carefully tear the packet and leave the tab attached to your shorts. Put solid fuel sources in a snack-size baggie and pin only one side of it to the inside of your waistband for easy access to calories midrun.[7]

5 STEPS TO FINDING YOUR PERFECT SPORTS BRA[8]

If you think you've already found it, you may be wrong—experts say that as many as 80 percent of women exercise in sports bras that aren't right for their body type. You may just not know what "perfect" feels like until you follow these tips.

1. **TRY LOTS OF SIZES AND STYLES.** Just as your street-shoe size may be different from your running-shoe size, your sports-bra size may be different from your everyday-bra size. (And unless you've been fitted, you're likely wearing the wrong size in those, too.) Because your breasts can change so much over time, never assume you know your size.

2. **CHECK THE STRAPS.** They should be resting against your skin without digging in or gapping. If you can comfortably fit two fingers (but no more) beneath each strap, you're on the right track. A tighter or looser fit will lead to chafing and/or subpar support.

3. **CHECK THE BAND.** You should only be able to fit one finger beneath the band if the bra's fitting properly.

4. **ASSESS THE FABRIC.** It should be lying smooth against your skin. Any wrinkles, gathers, or pulled areas indicate an improper fit.

5. **MOVE AROUND.** If all else looks good, jog in place in the dressing room and observe how the bra feels during movement. Consider doing some jumping jacks or hops to see how it holds up during higher-impact activities. Better yet, if you're at a specialty store with a treadmill, ask to try the bra on a short run.

4 ANSWERS TO THE QUESTION "WHAT'S THE POINT OF COMPRESSION GEAR?" . . . [9]

Some runners are really into supertight (and often superexpensive) socks, tights, and sleeves. If you're wondering if you should be, too, here are some reasons people wear it.

1. **IT MAKES THEM FEEL FASTER.** No research has shown that wearing squeezy apparel midrun helps or hinders performance. But some runners like the way compression apparel looks and feels on the run.

2. **IT ADDS SOME WARMTH.** Sometimes a crisp fall day will be too warm for tights but a little too cool for shorts alone. Enter the shorts-with-compression-socks look. One caveat: It's not wise to layer compression gear (e.g., socks beneath compression tights).

3. **IT BOOSTS RECOVERY.** There is research to support the connection between wearing compression gear postrun and decreased soreness. Tight gear can boost circulation, and you get the added psychological benefit of feeling like you're doing something to promote healing. This only works if you have the right fit, though, so read packaging carefully—compression gear isn't one-size-fits-all.

4. **IT MAKES FOR SAFER FLYING.** Even nonrunners might wear compression socks on a plane to promote blood flow and lower the risk of developing a blood clot. This is especially smart to do postrace, when your muscles are already damaged and you may be dehydrated (which can increase your clot risk).

. . . AND 1 COMPRESSION CAVEAT[10]

While medical compression gear is FDA regulated, compression gear for runners is not. In order for compression socks or sleeves to work as advertised, the product should provide the most compression in the ankle area, with the compression getting lighter and lighter moving up toward the calf area. According to an independent study commissioned by the compression company CEP, many brands flip this: They're tighter at the top and looser on the bottom. These "upside-down" socks can be ineffective, or worse, they may cause blood to pool in the feet.

FIFTEEN

OTHER STUFF

---

5 REASONS CHEAP TREADMILLS
ARE SO CHEAP . . . [1]

We said "cheap" instead of "inexpensive" for a reason--new machines that cost less than four figures (and especially those under $500) are not typically built to last. Here's where the "savings" come from.

1. **WEAK MOTORS.** The engines on lower-quality 'mills must run all-out to keep you running, which can cause a burning smell that means, "This machine isn't long for this world!"
2. **CRUMMY WIRING.** Cheap wires may not be able to handle the demands of a weak motor that's constantly going at full power. Cue more burning smell.
3. **PLASTIC GEARS.** These change the incline on cheap treadmills and are far less durable than the steel gears on higher-end models.
4. **SLOW PROCESSORS.** You'll feel more jerks and sudden shifts when trying to change the speed settings on a cheap treadmill.

5. **SHODDY COMPONENTS.** Cheap machines use plastic bearing caps instead of steel on the rollers, which makes them more prone to breakdown.

. . . AND 6 TIPS FOR BUYING A USED MACHINE[2]

Just because you're on a budget doesn't mean your only option is a subpar treadmill that may or may not last a complete training cycle. Someone else's loss of motivation to exercise more regularly can be your gain—if you follow these guidelines.

1. **FIND A REPUTABLE BRAND.** Don't buy from someone who cheaped out. You'll want a model that would cost at least $1,000 new. Google the brand name and, if available, the model name. An archive of our reviews can be found at runnersworld.com/treadmills.

2. **ASK THE RIGHT QUESTIONS.** In an ideal situation, you'd be buying from the only owner and user, who stored the treadmill in a dry place and is selling because he or she just doesn't use it.

3. **GET THE HISTORY.** Find out if and when the treadmill has been serviced previously and what the issue was.

4. **WHEN POSSIBLE, GO NEWER.** A machine that's less than 5 years old is ideal—but wear and tear matters more than age. Choose a 6-year-old, barely touched machine over a newer one that's been used daily.

5. **TEST IT OUT.** Run on it for at least 20 to 30 minutes. If it's loud, shaky, or gives off the burning smell of a cheap or broken treadmill, keep looking.

BONUS TIP Stick your GPS watch outside *before* your final prerun bathroom break—it'll find satellites while you're on the can.

6. **BRING UP THE WARRANTY.** Used stores may offer one, or you may be able to transfer the warranty from a private seller.

10 THINGS TO CONSIDER WHEN BUYING A JOGGING STROLLER[3,4]

As if bouncing back from pregnancy weren't physically demanding enough, some women add pushing their young child to the mix. There are perks for everyone, but the wrong stroller can mean the difference between "challenging" and "impossible." Here's what first-timers should evaluate before committing.

1. **CONVERTIBILITY.** A jogging stroller is just an ordinary stroller with three wheels instead of four, and with a cushier ride. Your other option is a pod that can be adapted for running, cycling, or a handful of other sports.

2. **HANDLEBAR HEIGHT.** You want the handlebar to be easy to grip when your elbows are bent about 90 degrees. One that adjusts is ideal if you and your partner are runners of different heights.

3. **WHEELS.** Make sure they're at least 16 inches in diameter for optimal handling. Some models allow you to lock the front

wheel to keep the stroller moving in a straight line without using both hands.

4. **BRAKES.** Some models have them; some don't. Steep downhills can be tough (and possibly dangerous) without brakes.

5. **AGE AND WEIGHT RATING.** Many models aren't suitable for babies younger than 6 months old, though some are approved even for newborns. Consider the upper weight limit if you

BONUS TIP[5] Stop wasting time on tangled headphone cords—and stop wrapping them around your device, because that'll eventually wear away at the cables. Instead, wrap the cord loosely around your fingers, leaving about 6 inches at the end. Pull the loop off your fingers and wrap the end of the cord loosely around that. Pull the headphone jack through, and store in a baggie until next time. Pull out the jack while holding the earbuds to unravel the whole cord, sans knots.

want to push your kids well into toddlerhood, since you'll want a model that will accommodate their increased weight.

6. **SEAT.** You may or may not be able to adjust the seat's position. Some come with extra padding, while others require you to pay more to add it.

7. **CANOPY.** How much protection does it offer from rain, sunshine, and wind? Depending on where you live, you may only need to worry about a couple of these variables.

8. **PORTABILITY.** Some jogging strollers can fold up really well—so you can use them as everyday strollers, too.

9. **PRICE.** The more features you want or need, the more you're likely to pay. Stake out Craigslist, eBay, or consignment shops to find good deals on costlier models.

10. **HOW IT FEELS.** This really is the most important factor. If at all possible, take a stroller for a test run, preferably with your child inside, before paying for it.

SIXTEEN

HEALTH, HYGIENE, AND APPEARANCE

THE 5-PRODUCT, HEAD-TO-TOE GUIDE
TO SUN PROTECTION

Unless you're a vampire, you're likely running outside between sunrise and sunset. If the sun's up—even if it's just after dawn, or cloudy, or wintertime—you're being exposed to UV rays that contribute to skin cancer.[1] Luckily, you can sport some relatively easy preventive measures.

1. **A HAT OR VISOR WITH A BRIM.** If you have short, parted, or no hair, a hat offers extra scalp protection.[2] Hats and visors for runners often have dark-colored material on the underside of the brim, which minimizes glare.
2. **SUNGLASSES.**[3] Find ones that offer 100 percent UV protection and don't slip or fog as you sweat. Lens color and polarization don't affect how well glasses filter rays, so choose whatever you like best.
3. **SUNSCREEN.** Try a few sweatproof options with an SPF of at least 30[4] to find which feels most comfortable during activity. If you're wearing a hat and sunglasses, you needn't put it on your forehead, and you'll avoid sunscreen running into your

eyes.[5] Make sure to get your neck, ears, and any other exposed skin. Use a shotglass-size amount of lotion to cover your body[6] and reapply every hour or two.

4. **LIP BALM WITH SPF.** If you don't mind the flavor or sensation of sunscreen on your lips, you can use that, but a balm might be more palatable. Plus, you can easily carry the tube for frequent reapplication on this common skin-cancer site.[7]

5. **OPAQUE CLOTHING.** If you hold an article of clothing up to a light source and no light shines through, it'll protect the skin underneath it from the sun.[8]

5 WEIRD (BUT EFFECTIVE) CHAFE-STOPPERS[9]

In 2015, we asked followers of the *Runner's World* Facebook page how they prevent chafing. While plenty of people reported using balms and plastic bandages, others got creative.

1. **SARAN WRAP.** Place it under a sports-bra band or other secure hot spot to reduce friction.

2. **COCONUT OIL.** It's basically an all-natural, tropical-scented Body Glide.

3. **AN OLD SOCK.** Cut off the toe or foot and wear it beneath an armband to protect your skin from pinching.

4. **DUCT TAPE.** One fellow wears this on his nipples, citing that "taking it off after a run helps me toughen up." Hey, whatever works. It'd likely be effective beneath elastic bands as well.

5. **WEARING CLOTHES INSIDE OUT.** If you don't own seamless clothing or socks, turning clothes with seams inside out keeps the seams away from your skin.

4 MIDRUN MAKEUP TIPS (IF YOU WANT TO WEAR MAKEUP MIDRUN)[10]

If you prefer to log miles au naturel (except for sunscreen, because everyone should be wearing that!), cool—skip this section. Otherwise, here's how to avoid looking like your face is slowly melting off the moment you begin to sweat.

1. **START WITH SPF 30+ SUNSCREEN.** Just say no to skin cancer!

2. **AVOID OIL-BASED FOUNDATIONS.** To avoid clogged pores and trapped sweat, try a tinted moisturizer or water- or powder-based product. If you find one with a high enough SPF, you may be able to skip sunscreen—but only on the parts of your face the foundation covers. If you're not applying foundation to your neck, ears, or lips, they need SPF from another source.

3. **WATERPROOF YOUR EYES.** You'll want waterproof eyeliner and mascara to avoid the raccoon look. These products are often so long-wearing that they're hard to take off, so invest in a good quality makeup remover, too.

4. **HIT YOUR LIPS.** Lip stains and glosses, as well as tinted balms, are less likely to smear than most lipsticks. Try swigging from a water bottle or cup at home before attempting it during a run or race to make sure hydrating doesn't cause a mess.

> **BONUS TIP** If you've got long hair that slowly becomes a rat's nest as it swishes back and forth in a ponytail, detangle like a pro—leave your hair up and, using a soft-bristled brush or wide-toothed comb, start working on the last couple inches of your hair. Once those are knot-free, move a few inches up. Working from the bottom stops knots from forming.

> **BONUS TIP** If you have a lot of hair, dry shampoo will change your life. Spray some near your roots, brush and fluff your strands (maybe with a quick blast of cool air from a hair dryer), and boom: Your hair looks and smells as if you washed and dried it in a fraction of the time. Find a product without talc to avoid white flakes.[11]

5 TYPES OF SELF-MASSAGE TOOLS YOU MIGHT SEE (AND HOW TO KNOW WHICH TO CHOOSE)

"Self-myofascial release" is the technical term for DIY massage using tools to work out your own kinks, improve range of motion, and kickstart recovery.[12] You could have a closet full of hurts-so-good torture devices if you wanted, but if you just want to buy one or two, here's what each is best for.

1. **SMOOTH ROLLERS.**[13] These come in low, medium, and firm densities. Firmer rollers are more effective, if you can avoid clenching your muscles when the sensation gets intense. Opt for the firmest roller you can stand or start with a less-firm roller and work your way up.

2. **BUMPY ROLLERS.**[14] If even a firm roller feels like it's not doing it for you, these *really* get in there. The bumps are meant to dig into trigger points and stubborn knots.

3. **SHORT ROLLERS.**[15] These also come in a range of densities, and they're easier to manage when you're targeting a small area. They're also more travel-friendly—though you may get some questions at the airport no matter which of these tools you choose.

4. **STICKS.**[16] You'll find semiflexible and less flexible versions of these products, which you grip at either end, press into a muscle, and roll up and down. It's like a roller, but you use arm pressure instead of your body weight, which usually leads to a less intense sensation. A rolling pin can deliver a similar effect.

BONUS TIP Premenopausal lady runners: Consider investing in a menstrual cup, a flexible, reusable device you insert into your vagina to catch your flow during your period. Sure, it's a little hands-on. And it takes some practice to learn to use one. But once you do, they're far more leakproof than tampons, and they only need to be emptied every 8 to 12 hours.[17]

5. **BALLS.**[18] You can use a golf ball to gently roll the bottoms of your feet or a tennis ball to get into bony areas around the hips and glutes. Use a slightly larger foam ball just about anywhere—beware, though, as it's far more targeted and intense than a roller.[19]

3 WAYS FOR MEN TO AVOID RUNNING WITH THEIR JUNK OUT[20]

If you wear short shorts, you're at risk of having your nether parts pop out, where they may bob and dangle for all the world to see. Here's how to avoid indecent exposure.

1. **REPLACE YOUR SHORTS REGULARLY.** Elastic doesn't last forever, and the elastic in your shorts' liner is what keeps your private parts private. If you're hanging on to a weathered pair that has sentimental value, wear them only on your home treadmill.

2. **CHOOSE TIGHTS WHEN IT'S COLD.** Freezing temperatures

lead to numb skin, and if your parts are numb, it may take you longer to notice that they've escaped.

3. **LISTEN TO THE HECKLERS.** If it's too late and you *are* busting out, the people you encounter will let you know. Someone shouting "Put that away!" is pretty obvious, but it's important to pick up on subtler signals, too. If an approaching pedestrian shoots you a look of disgust or jaywalks across the street to avoid you, check yourself.

SEVENTEEN

GEAR FOR SPECIAL CONDITIONS

6 STEPS TO ENSURE A PLEASANT RUN IN A DOWNPOUR[1]

Few forecasts strike fear into the hearts of runners more than rain—especially the cold variety. But unless you're the Wicked Witch of the West, getting wet isn't going to kill you. You might even enjoy rain running if you suit up correctly.

1. **START WITH A HAT OR VISOR.** The brim will keep water out of your eyes.
2. **ADD LIGHT-TINTED SUNGLASSES.** They're like goggles for when you're more or less swimming on land. Apply an antifog lens cleaner to enhance visibility.
3. **PROTECT YOUR TORSO.** On cold, wet days, this may mean wearing a waterproof shell not made for running—these are less breathable but far more protective. On warmer days, a lightweight, rain-resistant running jacket or vest will do. In a pinch, use a trash bag with holes cut out for your head and arms. (This is a good, disposable option on race day when it's not supposed to rain the whole time.)
4. **CHOOSE TIGHT, DARK-COLORED, WICKING APPAREL.**

Tech fabric doesn't absorb water like cotton does. The tighter your clothing, the less likely it is to chafe, so break out that spandex blend. And if you don't want to give everyone a free show, stick to dark colors—light ones become see-through when wet.

5. **WICKING SOCKS ARE ESPECIALLY IMPORTANT.** Do you want each foot to turn into a giant blister? No? Then steer clear of cotton (or even lower-quality "wicking") socks. Reserve your finest foot coverings for rainy runs.

6. **YOU CAN'T USE TOO MUCH LUBE.** Coat your feet in petroleum jelly or Bag Balm (a superthick moisturizing product originally developed— seriously—for irritated cow udders) before slipping them into your luxurious socks. Use petroleum jelly or antichafing balm on any other potential hot spots: between your thighs, under your arms, on your nipples, and beneath any seams.

> **BONUS TIP** The best way to dry out soaked shoes is to remove the sock liners and stuff the shoes with newspaper. (Who says print is dead?)[2]

7 WAYS TO GEAR UP FOR WINTER[3]

There are plenty of reasons some runners abandon the sport in the darkest, coldest months: They're busy with the holidays. Their next race isn't until May. They're camped out beneath a quilt in their robes and their slippers and they refuse to emerge until the weather is mild again. Still, winter is long, and it feels longer when you're not outside being active. Suit up properly and you can run safely in most wintry conditions.

1. **DON'T OVERDRESS . . .** You heat up as you run, so dress as if it were about 10 degrees warmer than it is. You want to feel cold when you step outside, but comfortable once you've

completed about a mile. When in doubt, visit runnersworld.com/what towear for help.

BONUS TIP Don't mess with ice: If there's a fresh coating from freezing rain, hit the treadmill.

2. **. . . BUT PROTECT YOUR EXTREMITIES . . .** Your hands and ears might not warm up as well as the rest of your body, especially if it's windy or precipitating. Wear gloves and a headband, hat, or earmuffs. You can always stuff 'em in a pocket if you get too warm.

3. **. . . AND YOUR FACE.** Sunglasses help prevent dry eyes in winter's dry air, and you'll still need protection from the sun, even when it doesn't seem bright. On really cold days, a buff you can pull over your mouth and nose can help your airways stay moist and warm.

4. **INVEST IN PETROLEUM JELLY.** Rub it on your lips and around your nose to avoid chapping.

5. **WEAR LAYERS.** Start with a wicking T-shirt and build from there. Vests are nice for chilly days; save jackets for when it's downright cold. Shorts over tights, while not exactly fashion-forward, can provide extra wind protection for your buns and privates. If you're not sure whether you're dressed right, plan a looped or figure-eight route to drop extra stuff at your home or car as you warm up.

6. **WEAR LIGHTS.** If any part of your run will take place in the dark, moving lights help drivers see you. Lights that you hold in your hands or attach to your shoes are good, as are head-lamps or "taillights" that blink. Reflective or neon gear doesn't hurt, but always have lights.

7. **GET A GRIP.** On snowy runs, consider trail shoes or traction devices that slip over your regular shoes. You can also make your own grippy shoes by taking an old pair and drilling short screws into the soles; see a demonstration at runnersworld.com /shoespikes.

7 THINGS YOU'LL WANT IF YOU GET REALLY INTO TRAIL RUNNING[4]

Trail runners are known for having a more laid-back vibe than roadies. That's what spending time in nature—far from car exhaust, distracted drivers, and other road hazards—will do for you. Here's how to look (and feel) the part.

1. **TRAIL SHOES.** These have grippier treads than road shoes, and the uppers tend to be made of material that's more resistant to water and dirt. Both are nice features to have when you're on really technical (and possibly muddy) terrain.[5]

2. **HIGH SOCKS.** Socks that rise above your ankles help keep crap out of your shoes. Gaiters, which go over your shoes and ankles, work even better.

3. **LIGHTWEIGHT TOPS AND BOTTOMS WITH MORE COVERAGE.** Tiny shorts and singlets leave a lot of skin exposed to sun, poisonous plants, and potentially disease-carrying bugs that multiply in natural environments.

4. **HEAVY-DUTY BUG REPELLENT.** Apply permethrin to shoes, socks, and other trail gear to kill more than 50 kinds of insects (including ticks, mosquitoes, and flies) on contact. Just keep it away from pets—it's especially toxic to cats.

5. **A HYDRATION SYSTEM.** Truly out-there trails aren't going to have plumbing, which means no flush toilets or water fountains, so bring enough fluids to last the length of your run. A handheld might hold enough. A hydration pack with a bladder is a better bet for longer, warmer efforts.

6. **A MAP.** You may not get cell-phone service where you're going, so make sure you know your way in and out before you get started.

7. **A TRUCKER HAT.** A lot of trail runners seem to wear these. Conform!

EIGHTEEN

PURGING GEAR

---

4 TYPES OF GEAR AND EQUIPMENT YOU SHOULD GTFO OF YOUR HOME[1]

We know, we know. It's hard to find time to sort through all your stuff when you're so busy logging miles, strength training, and doing all the other things *Runner's World* says you should do to perform your best. Start the purge with these items, as they could actually be *hindering* your fitness.

1. **BUSTED GADGETS.** If your iPod dies after 30 minutes no matter how long you've been charging it, or if you spend a run cramming your earbuds back in after they wriggle loose over and over again, that detracts from your workout. Recycle electronics that bug you and replace them with ones that actually work.

2. **AS-SEEN-ON-TV CONTRAPTIONS.** That Ab-Tron 3000 you ordered from QVC in 1999? Yeah, planks and side planks are more effective, and they don't require any machinery. Ditch anything you wouldn't find in a modern gym—free weights, bands, and Swiss balls are all A-OK to keep.

3. **OLD WATER BOTTLES.** Get rid of ones that are uncomfortable to tote on a run, leak, or don't fit in the cup holder on your treadmill. You really don't need more than one or two.

4. **CHEAP SUNGLASSES.** The shades you got for free at a work conference may not offer the recommended 99 to 100 percent protection from UV rays, and that's half the point of wearing them. Maybe keep them in your car as an emergency backup pair for better visibility, but otherwise, they belong in the recycling bin.

4 STEPS FOR THINNING OUT YOUR COLLECTION OF RUNNING CRAP[2]

Run for long enough, and you'll end up with infinity race tees, bibs, medals, hats, socks, gloves, pint glasses, and other memorabilia emblazoned with not-always-well-designed event logos. And that's *before* considering your pile o' running shoes. If you've amassed enough to qualify for *Hoarders: Runners' Edition*, here's how to lighten your load.

1. **START BY SORTING.** Divide race tees into a pile you actually like to wear and a pile of ill-fitting, ugly, or otherwise undesirable ones. Do the same with running shoes, but create three piles: still in rotation, completely worn out, and gently used pairs you don't really care for. Split medals into an "attractive and/or from races you look back upon fondly" pile and a "meh" pile. Consider bibs carefully: If you keep a medal, do you need to keep the bib too?

2. **MAKE MEMORIES FROZEN IN TIME.** Photograph each race's tee, medal, and bib together to put toward a scrapbook. You can caption those photos with details from the race, add any other race images you might have, and ditch the physical mementos.

3. **OR GET CRAFTIER.** If you can sew, make a blanket from old race tees—or pay someone else to do it. Bibs, medals, and race

photos from truly special events can be assembled into shadow boxes.

4. **GIVE TO CHARITY.** Shirts, hats, nearly new shoes, and other swag can be donated to Goodwill or the Salvation Army. Several organizations accept race-medal donations, and others recycle old shoes—Google to peruse your options. There's not much you can do with bibs, so send those to the recycling bin.

SECTION 4

158 MOTIVATION TIPS

THE 4 GOLDEN RULES OF MOTIVATION

1. **MEET A FRIEND.** You'll be doubly accountable to any given run if you have someone waiting for you. Plus, the run itself will be more enjoyable with company.
2. **TRY SOMETHING NEW.** Explore an unfamiliar neighborhood, a just-constructed bike path, or a mountain trail you've never visited. Variety is the spice of life—and running.
3. **BET ON YOURSELF.** Shelling out cash—for a race entry, some new running shoes, or the headlamp and reflective gear that'll crush your excuses for not getting out early—will encourage you to reap rewards from your investment.
4. **JUST DO IT.** Sometimes the only solution is sheer willpower. But the more times you exercise it, the less you'll need. Running feels less optional as you develop a habit of doing it regularly.

NINETEEN

GETTING OUT THE DOOR

---

9 TACTICS FOR BUSTING OUT OF A RUNNING RUT[1]

"Rut" sounds so negative, like something you tripped and fell into and need to claw your way out of. Instead, think of ruts as opportunities to freshen up your routine and become fitter and faster than ever.

1. **GO SOCIAL.** If you usually run alone, hook up with a friend or a group. If you do occasionally run with others, find new people to accompany you. Making friends takes your mind off the miles.

2. **TRY A NEW DISTANCE.** If you usually race 5Ks, set your sights on something longer. And if you're stuck in the grind of nonstop long-distance training, spend a training cycle or two targeting something short and fast.

3. **SHIFT YOUR SCENERY.** If you always race locally, plan a "race-cation." On the flip side, if you're always traveling to events, you may be more likely to hit a fast time when you can train on the course, prep your own prerace meals, and sleep in your own bed the night before.

4. **GET RIPPED.** Swap out a couple of runs for total-body strength sessions, on your own or as part of a class. Strong muscles help running feel easier. (You'll look better naked, too.)

5. **CHANGE DIRECTIONS.** Try some of your usual routes in reverse. You'll notice different scenery and *feel* like you're covering a new route, but you'll know how far you're going and avoid getting lost.

6. **HIT THE TRAILS.** Running on trails with rocks and roots is a completely different experience than logging miles on smooth roads. You'll also enjoy quiet time in nature, build coordination, and strengthen your stabilizing muscles.

7. **RACE LESS (OR NOT AT ALL).** Break your year into seasons—winter, spring, summer, and fall—and limit half- or full-marathon training to one or two of those seasons. If that doesn't excite you, wait for a goal that inspires you. You can run for fun and fitness without capital-T Training.

8. **PLAN A GETAWAY.** Many pro athletes, training groups, and other running organizations host camps or retreats meant to bring runners together and rejuvenate their routines. If you can't find one in your area, do it yourself: Rent a house with a few running buddies near roads or trails you're all excited to log miles on.

9. **RUN LESS.** Sometimes a rut is your body's way of crying uncle. Take a few weeks to do the bare minimum to maintain fitness—about 30 minutes

BONUS TIP Two of the toughest times of year for runners are when it starts getting warm (and then downright hot) and the frantic holiday season. To stay on the wagon, join a #RWRunStreak. One runs from Memorial Day (the last Monday in May) through the Fourth of July; the other, from American Thanksgiving (the third Thursday in November) through New Year's Day. You run at least 1 mile every day and, if you want, track your progress on social media using #RWRunStreak. Learn more at runnersworld.com/streak.

of easy running, about every other day. Or just don't maintain your fitness—you can always get it back. Other cardio training, such as swimming, cycling, or group classes, can keep your heart and lungs ready to run.

4 SITUATIONS THAT'LL SAP YOUR MOTIVATION (AND WHETHER YOU SHOULD RUN ANYWAY)[2]

There's a reason that, in most pop-culture portrayals, the fastest zombies can move is a brisk lurch: When you're feeling dead on your feet, the last thing you want to do is run. Sometimes, though, a few miles will bring you back to life. Here's how to know when you should *World War Z* it and when you should just stay in the crypt.

1. **YOU SLEPT POORLY.** A short run is a cold shower in exercise form: It may be unpleasant at first, but you'll likely feel more alert when you return. If you've been tossing and turning for several nights, and you have the opportunity to sleep in, do it. But if you're, say, a new parent, and sleeping in isn't an option, keep up regular running to feel more human.

2. **YOU FEEL SOMETHING COMING ON.** Generally, sleep will help you fend off a cold or other bug better than running will. You might still be able to run later in the day—see "The 4 Rules of Running (or Resting) While Sick" (page 184) for guidelines.

3. **YOU'RE SO BUSY.** A short, easy run can help you burn off some anxiety, so take 30 minutes to jog around at the start or end of a stressful day.

4. **YOU'RE SO SORE.** If your body's crying out after a new cross-training workout or big race, a very short, very gentle run (or run-walk) might help you recover more quickly. If, however, the discomfort causes you to alter your gait, take a rest day—you don't want to hurt yourself.

6 MANTRAS TO REPEAT WHEN YOU JUST DON'T WANT TO RUN

Stick one to your alarm clock. Tape one up on your bathroom mirror. Affix another to your coffeemaker. And watch your excuses keel over and die.

1. "I don't have to run. I *get* to run."
2. "The only run you regret is the one you don't go on."[3]
3. "To run is a privilege, not a chore."[4]
4. "Every run is a gift."[5]
5. "There's no such thing as a bad run."[6]
6. "Run for those who can't."[7]

5 WAYS TO MAKE IT HARDER TO SKIP AN EVENING RUN[8]

If you wait until the end of a busy day to get out the door, you must overcome mental fatigue. It's possible to be zonked even if you've been deskbound because of drops in the brain chemicals that make you feel energized. And there are just so many other things you might need or want to do: cooking dinner, meeting a friend for drinks, putting on sweatpants and flopping onto the couch. How does anyone manage to postpone much-needed sweatpants time? These tactics help.

BONUS TIP A 2017 study found that each hour you run grants you about 7 hours of additional longevity.[9] How's *that* for motivation?

1. **HAVE A SNACK.** If you've barely eaten since lunch, your blood sugar could be low. A couple graham crackers or half a banana will work wonders. Keep a stash of easy-to-digest options in your desk, locker, or gym bag.

2. **CHANGE AT WORK (OR SCHOOL).** Waiting until you're inside your home (with all its nonrunning temptations) is unwise.

3. **LEAVE FROM WORK (OR SCHOOL).** Or stop at a park off your commute route. Or park outside your home and depart without going in. Again: Once you're in that door, it's harder.

4. **MEET OTHER PEOPLE.** Friends are best: They'll be mad if you bail. Failing that, connect with your local running club or specialty store—they likely offer weekly group runs that are free to join.

5. **REMEMBER THE PAYOFF.** If you're only mentally fatigued, know that running provides a boost that can help you do whatever else you need to do before bedtime.

TWENTY

MIDRUN TROUBLESHOOTING

10 WAYS TO TOUGH OUT A MISERABLE RUN[1]

Motivation that gets you out the door is one thing. If you're struggling once you're out there—and you're miles from home when the "sufferfest" begins—these tactics can help you complete your run in one piece.

1. **THINK SMALL.** Break down the remainder of your run into small chunks and conquer them one by one. You may think "just one more mile" even if there are more miles to go, or think even smaller, choosing a landmark up ahead to run to and choosing another once you pass it.
2. **USE A MANTRA.** Studies show positive ones ("I'm feeling great!") work better than negative ones ("don't give up!"),[2] but we're all different. If "stop being such a wimp!" works for you, go with it.
3. **ENVISION SUCCESS.** Picture a competitor, like a local road-race rival or annoying coworker, and imagine *them* stopping to walk or slowing down as you cruise ahead. You, for the win!
4. **TRY FORM CUES.** Tell yourself to run tall or claw the ground to avoid slumping or shuffling as you fatigue. Or you can time

your inhales and exhales to your footfalls—the synchronicity can be hypnotic.

BONUS TIP Know the difference between a tough run and an injury. If you're feeling any sharp, localized pain that causes you to alter your gait, slow to a walk or call for a ride.

5. **INDULGE POSTRUN DAYDREAMS.** What are you going to do after you've conquered this run? Perhaps there's a hot bath, a long nap, or a giant stack of pancakes in your future. Imagine how great *that's* going to be.

6. **TUNE IN.** If you're wearing headphones, now is the time to employ your favorite pump-up jams. If not, use the DJ in your head: Play the theme from *Chariots of Fire*, "Eye of the Tiger," or another, less ubiquitous motivational earworm.

7. **EXERCISE YOUR MIND.** Count your footfalls, add them together, multiply them, or do other mental math for the sake of distraction. If you're bilingual without being fluent, try translating all your thoughts into the other language.

8. **BE SELF-CONSCIOUS.** Now is a good time to start caring what people think: Try to imagine how embarrassing it would be to be seen walking home or to ask that gas station cashier to use their phone to call for a ride.

9. **KEEP PERSPECTIVE.** Logging a few more miles isn't as hard as giving birth, undergoing major surgery, or going through a divorce. If you've endured something truly tough, use your memories of that time to fuel your resolve.

10. **BE GRATEFUL.** If you're out running at all, you're blessed with a body that can do it and the time to take care of yourself. Someday you'll no longer be able to run, but today is not that day.

5 MANTRAS TO MAKE A TOUGH RUN FEEL EASIER

Research shows that focusing on a positive phrase can help you run faster for longer—and struggle less while you're doing it. Try these on for size and keep them in your pocket for when you're struggling to stay the course.

> **BONUS TIP** Before a long run or race, think of 5 to 10 people (or animals, or causes) you care about and plan to dedicate one of your last miles to each of them.[8]

1. "Run the mile you're in."[3]
2. "Stay relaxed, stay calm."[4]
3. "Light and smooth."[5]
4. "Everything forward."[6]
5. "Think strong, be strong, finish strong."[7]

4 WAYS TO MAKE THE MOST OF SOLO RUNS[9]

You can't rely on always having company. Otherwise, you may never log miles when you or your running buddy are out of town. What if the apocalypse arrives and you're the only surviving runner? Here's how to avoid a slump when you must go it alone.

1. **MIX UP DISTANCE AND PACE.** Faster and longer runs may be easier to do with company, but they're critical for building fitness. So if you mostly train solo, designate at least one hard-effort and one long-effort day per week (Track Tuesday, Long Run Saturday) and make nailing those workouts your priority.

2. **FIND A (VIRTUAL) FRIEND.** Technology makes it easy to connect with buddies even if you're not near enough to run together. If you sign up for a race with a faraway friend, the two of you can exchange updates postrun as a way of holding each other accountable.

3. **BANISH BOREDOM.** Mix up your routes as much as possible— leave from home some days, from work others, and head to different parks on the weekends. And in lieu of stimulating conversation with another human on the run, let your mind wander. Envision success at your upcoming race, plan your

BONUS TIP Before cell phones, if you wanted to bail on a run, you needed to find a pay phone and call collect to ask someone to pick you up. It's nice to have a phone with you in case of emergency, but if you find yourself using it regularly to call a ride, take multiple selfie breaks, or have an excuse to stop whenever you get a notification, start leaving it behind.

next big trip, or stew over long-simmering resentments. Hey, it all helps pass the time!

4. **REMEMBER: YOU'RE THE BOSS.** If you have to stop to poop, you can take your time. If you didn't sleep well and you're dragging ass, you're not holding anyone back. Sometimes, focusing on what's great about running solo can help it feel like less of a chore.

6 WAYS TO DIY A RUNNER'S HIGH[10, 11]

If a runner's high were a sure thing, there would be a whole lot more runners on the roads and trails. Unfortunately, not every outing results in euphoric feelings. Still, there are some things you can do to make each run as enjoyable as possible—and "enjoyable" is the first step on the path to "whoaaaaaaa, look at that tree, man, it's so beautiful."

1. **SCHEDULE SMART.** If you're rushing to complete your run before dashing off to work or prepping dinner, you won't have fun. Create ample space in your day to log your miles, and

avoid cutting it close. If you only *might* be able to squeeze in 5, do 3 or 4 instead.

2. **TAKE IT EASY . . .** Spend a little time easing into and out of your run by walking or doing some dynamic stretching, and try cruising at a conversational pace. At this effort level, your body produces endocannabinoids, a natural version of the component in marijuana responsible for its high.

3. **. . . OR RAMP IT UP.** Endorphins, the feel-good chemicals your body releases in response to discomfort or pain, are best generated by a sustained, comfortably challenging effort, like a tempo run.

4. **JOIN A GROUP . . .** Research suggests that exercising with others may stimulate a greater endorphin release than running alone.

5. **. . . OR FIND SOLO BLISS.** Listening to your favorite jams might also induce endorphins—just make sure you're still aware of your surroundings. If you're a runner who prefers to go without gadgets, tuning in to the sights, sounds, and smells of nature can have a similar effect.

6. **THINK POSITIVE.** Check in with your form every mile or so to make sure you're not holding tension in your neck or shoulders, and say to yourself, "Wow, I feel good." Where the mind goes, the body tends to follow.

TWENTY-ONE

ENLISTING HELP

---

4 WAYS TO FIND A RUNNING BUDDY

If you're the only runner in your social network, you have two problems: One is that you'll have to come up with a good response to "running will ruin your knees!" The second is that you'll have no one to turn to when you don't feel like slogging it out alone. Luckily, there are many ways to connect with the community.

1. **JOIN GROUP RUNS.** If you're a regular at your local club's Wednesday night 4-miler, you'll get to know the other regulars over time. Once you've built a rapport with those who are about your pace, you can suggest meeting up to run on other days.
2. **ATTEND RUNNING EVENTS.** If your local club or specialty store hosts speakers, shoe company presentations, or wine-and-cheese mixers, go: You may get chatting with someone who's training for the same race you are or who's new to the area.
3. **VOLUNTEER.** Helping out at races in your hometown isn't just good karma—it's an opportunity to expand your network. Choose posts with some downtime, like packet pickup or T-shirt distribution, over action-packed duties to have a chance to converse.
4. **TURN TO THE INTERNET.** A local running club or race's

Facebook page may include posts from other runners seeking company. (If you go this route, meet for the first time in a well-populated public place—basic Internet safety!) And at least one relay series (Ragnar) has a tool that connects teams that are short a runner to people looking to join teams.[1]

3 TIMES YOU CAN USE MUSIC TO RUN BETTER

If you've ever felt a surge of adrenaline upon hearing the opening drumbeats of Springsteen's "Born to Run" while waiting to start a race, you already know that what you hear has a direct effect on how you feel—and how pumped you are to perform. It's the reason that five volumes of *Jock Jams* exist. But music has a place in the leadup to race day, too.

1. **BEFORE A RUN.** A 2014 study found that listening to pump-up jams before a hard run affects the brain in a way that readies it to perform.[2] The research used songs in the 110 to 150 beats-per-minute (bpm) range; "Born to Run" has 147.[3]

2. **DURING A RUN.** Believe it or not, the same study found that runners who listened to slow music (80 to 100 bpm) as they ran finished a 5K time trial *faster* than those who listened to fast music (140 to 160 bpm).[4] However, earlier research found that the harder your effort level, the less of a performance effect music has, so it might be wise to tune in to your body when pushing the pace. If you're doing an interval workout, spend your recovery periods listening to slow-tempo music (100 to 120 bpm) to ready yourself for the next rep, then pause the tunes before taking off.[5]

3. **AFTER A RUN.** Research from 2016 found that listening to similarly slow-tempo music after a hard treadmill workout helped runners' heart rates return to baseline more quickly than fast music or white noise.[6] It's worth using during active recovery *and* postrun—so build up that playlist of 100- to 120-bpm jams.

135 | ENLISTING HELP

FIFTEEN 100- TO 120-BPM SONGS THAT JUST ABOUT EVERYONE KNOWS[7]

Here, we started your playlist for you.

"I Walk the Line" by Johnny Cash
"Work It" by Missy Elliott
"Edge of Seventeen" by Stevie Nicks
"Eye of the Tiger" by Survivor
"With a Little Help from My Friends" by the Beatles
"I Feel Good" by James Brown
"Another One Bites the Dust" by Queen
"Breakfast at Tiffany's" by Deep Blue Something
"Let's Get It Started" by the Black Eyed Peas
"Jungle Boogie" by Kool & the Gang
"More Than a Feeling" by Boston
"Livin' on a Prayer" by Bon Jovi
"I Wanna Dance with Somebody" by Whitney Houston
"Thriller" by Michael Jackson
"Semi-Charmed Life" by Third Eye Blind

7 STRATEGIES FOR RUNNING WITH YOUR SIGNIFICANT OTHER[8]

If you're reading this section, you've likely had a few unpleasant runs with your partner. Welcome to the club: Even if you and your favorite person both love to run, you may not have yet discovered a way to love running *together*. Try to make it happen with these tactics.

1. **GET ON THE SAME PAGE.** Your comfortable pace may not be the same as your partner's. If you're trying to stick together, let the slower partner lead—and if you are that person, speak up as soon as the pace gets too challenging.

2. **AND STAY THERE, PEACEFULLY.** Just as they are in life, in running, "I statements" are the key to making your feelings known without pissing anyone off. For example, instead of "You're going too fast," say "I need to slow down."

3. **DON'T "HELP."** Now's not the time for unsolicited advice, especially if you're gliding along no problem while your partner is huffing and puffing.

4. **SAVE TOUGH CONVOS FOR LATER.** Now's also not the time to bring up that thing you were arguing about earlier. Fighting while flighting is a recipe for a bad experience.

5. **MAKE A RACE-DAY PLAN.** If you're racing together, agree ahead of time whether you'll stick together at all costs or split up if one person feels like going ahead or falling behind. Know what kind of motivational talk works for your partner: Some people respond well to "This guy is coming up behind you, pick it up!" while other people *really* don't.

6. **TRY DOING YOUR OWN THING.** You don't have to be together the whole time. Try warming up and cooling down with your partner, or having the faster partner run ahead for a while before doubling back to meet the slower partner.

7. **DON'T FORCE IT.** Even if you're both runners, you don't have to run together. As long as you enjoy being together when you're *not* running, your relationship is sound.

11 THINGS TO KNOW ABOUT RUNNING WITH YOUR DOG[9]

If humans were always as excited as dogs to leave the house and get some exercise, we'd solve the obesity crisis (and maybe even achieve world peace). People aren't quite as energetic, but the enthusiasm of your pooch can be contagious, and that's why you may be tempted to run with him. How do you make it happen? Read on.

1. **ALL BREEDS ARE DIFFERENT.** Retrievers, Dalmatians, German shepherds, and terriers are natural runners, while dogs on either end of the size spectrum like tiny Chihuahuas and enormous mastiffs are not. When in doubt, ask your vet whether trying a run is appropriate.

2. **WAIT UNTIL HE'S MATURE.** This means 12 months old for smaller dogs and 18 for larger breeds. Again, talk to your vet if you're not sure.

3. **GET THE RIGHT GEAR.** Avoid retractable leashes for running, since they can tangle and your dog can easily get away from you if he spots something interesting. Invest in a hands-free leash that attaches to your waist if you'll be running long or often with your pup. Your dog should wear either a head-collar or harness.

4. **POOP FIRST.** Your dog likely associates the leash with an opportunity to pop a squat. Do this as part of your walking warmup and circle back to your home or a trash can to discard the turd bag.

5. **WORK YOUR WAY UP.** Dogs need to ease into a running program just as humans do. If you've been going on regular walks, try 15 minutes of running, three times a week. Once your dog is cool with that, you can add 5 minutes to each run each week.

6. **CHOOSE THE RIGHT ROUTE.** You want your first routes to be relatively flat, without much car and pedestrian traffic. Avoid steamy asphalt or anywhere that may have broken glass or other hazards that can hurt your pal's paws.

7. **BE PATIENT.** It takes time to sync up with your dog, who might be more interested in peeing on every landmark than maintaining a consistent pace. This can improve with practice.

8. **GIVE HIM SOME SLACK.** When teaching your dog to run, keep him about 3 feet from you, with some wiggle room in the leash.

9. **BRING WATER FOR BOTH OF YOU . . .** Otherwise, your dog will lap up whatever's available—and you don't know what's in the puddles of runoff on the street.

10. **. . . AND TREATS FOR HIM.** If you reward your dog for ignoring a squirrel and continuing to run, he's more likely to ignore them in the future.

11. **LISTEN TO YOUR DOGGY.** He can't tell you when he's tired, so watch for excessive panting. You may notice his mouth curled back, or that his breathing doesn't return to normal quickly during a break. If this happens, slow to a walk and head home.

TWENTY-TWO

SHELLING OUT

---

6 QUESTIONS TO ASK A COACH
BEFORE YOU COMMIT[1]

This is it: You're ready to spend some serious cash to have someone else plan your training. Maybe your performance has plateaued, or you can't manage to arrive at a starting line without some kind of debilitating injury. Having a coach can change your life—*if* you find the right person. Here's what to ask before you make a final decision.

1. **WHAT'S YOUR EDUCATIONAL BACKGROUND?** Ideally, you'll find someone with a degree in physiology, anatomy, kinesiology, or exercise science. Anyone can sign up for coaching certification programs, but the most qualified coaches have more credentials.

2. **HOW MANY RUNNERS LIKE ME HAVE YOU COACHED?** You want your coach to have experience training runners of your age and ability level for your goal distance.

3. **WHAT'S YOUR COACHING PHILOSOPHY?** You'll want to be on roughly the same page. For example, if the coach believes it's best to train by effort level and time and you're a die-hard data junkie, you're a poor match.

4. **WHAT'S YOUR EXPERI-ENCE WORKING WITH INDIVIDUALS?** It takes a different skill set to prepare a running club or a group of charity runners for an event than to deliver personalized attention.

> **BONUS TIP** Save a dollar in a jar for every mile you run. Once it's full, treat yo'self to something special—a race registration, a sports massage, or that fancy gadget you've been coveting.

5. **HOW MUCH PERSONAL INTERACTION CAN I EXPECT TO HAVE?** Find out how the coach prefers to communicate (phone? e-mail? text?) and how often you can expect to hear from him or her. If you want more access than the coach is able to provide, keep searching.

6. **WHAT'S YOUR BACKGROUND IN DEALING WITH INJURY?** If you have a history of problems, it's especially important to hire someone with an exercise science or kinesiology background who can assess your strength and flexibility.

11 STRATEGIES FOR RACING ON THE CHEAP[2]

Nothing boosts motivation like having a race on the calendar. But if you don't believe a half-day event ought to cost more than a year's worth of running shoes, there are ways to compete without depleting your funds.

1. **RACE LESS.** Sounds obvious, but a chronic racing habit gets expensive, and you're not likely to deliver peak performances if you line up too often anyway. Limit yourself to one or two half or full marathons per year. If you race 5Ks, choose about four per year to target as goals.
2. **RACE LOCALLY.** You'll save on transportation, lodging, and food by doing the race in your backyard instead of the exciting destination event. Plus, you'll be able to train on the course—a big advantage.

3. **REGISTER SO EARLY . . .** Generally, the further in advance you sign up for a race, the better a deal you'll get.

4. **. . . OR SO LATE.** If you miss the early-bird price breaks and a race allows it, signing up on-site at the expo or on race day can save you the online registration fee. (Obviously, this won't work for sell-out races.)

5. **WIELD THE POWER OF THE INTERNET.** Follow a race you want to run on social media—events often offer limited-time discount codes to boost registration numbers. And Google your race and its organizers in advance to avoid wasting your cash on a subpar, disorganized event.

6. **FORGET FRILLS.** Old-school races without timing chips, finishers' medals, or postrace parties tend to be far cheaper than events with more production value. Heck, some are even free.

7. **OPT OUT.** Some races allow you to pay less to enter if you choose not to receive the swag.

8. **BECOME A VOLUNTEER.** Some organizers offer discounted or free entry to a future race in exchange for helping out at an event.

9. **BECOME AN AMBASSADOR.** If you have a big online following, some races will comp your entry in exchange for publicity. If you don't have one, it's free, if time-intensive, to try to build one.

10. **GET FASTER.** Some races comp elite or sub-elite runners. Others offer discounts if you're among the speedy set. If you're always winning your age group anyway, this is worth looking into.

11. **TALK TO HR.** As more employers realize that healthy workers are more productive, more workplaces are offering wellness programs and discounts. You may be eligible for free or discounted race entries, or to be reimbursed when you register for an event. It can't hurt to ask!

---

14 TIPS FOR THE PERFECT "RACE-CATION"[3]

Running and traveling go hand in hand: You don't need to tote a lot of gear to burn off the indulgences you enjoy when you're exploring a new place's cuisine. And when your trip includes a race, you know you'll be able to log a decent number of miles without running out of fuel or getting hopelessly lost. Here's what you need to know before you book.

1. **CHOOSE YOUR RACE (AND YOUR GOAL) WISELY.** Remember that it's easier to set PRs near home, where you can cook your own food and sleep in your own bed. And it's hard to bounce back from really long races like marathons and still have enough energy to walk around and sightsee.

2. **PLAN FOR JET LAG.** You'll need about a day of rest after you arrive for every two time zones you cross.

3. **BOOK A FLIGHT.** You'll want to be able to stretch your legs—especially on your return trip—because staying stationary for too long increases your risk of dangerous blood clots.[4] Avoid window seats, and if you're able, shell out a little extra for a shorter direct flight.

4. **MAKE A PRERACE DINNER RESERVATION—STAT.** This is especially important if you're traveling to a large race, or to a smaller one in a town with only one Italian restaurant.

5. **KNOW BEFORE YOU GO.** If you may not have Internet access when you get to your destination, print or write down all the necessary info from the race site, including start time, start location, transportation options, and whether the race is marked in miles or kilometers.

6. **PACK SMART.** Put everything you need for race day either in your carry-on or on your body, in case your luggage gets lost. And it's a lot easier to roll a suitcase on wheels than to haul a heavy duffel.

7. **BYO SUPPLIES.** Depending on where you're going, it may be tough to find a running store or a pharmacy. Pack what you need to prevent and treat chafing, blisters, sunburn, diarrhea, and aches and pains, and bring your preferred midrace fuel.

8. **BYO SNACKS.** The stuff you can buy in airports and on airplanes is overpriced *and* not ideal for someone about to run a

race. Bring what you'd eat at home: fruit, veggies, nuts, and healthy bars. Carry an empty water bottle you can fill in the terminal.

9. **DRESS TO COMPRESS.** Wear compression socks on the plane—they help prevent the aforementioned dangerous blood clots.

10. **HYDRATE.** Drinking nonalcoholic beverages in flight promotes circulation and helps fight dehydration exacerbated by a plane's recirculated air. Plan to have a cup of water every 60 to 90 minutes.

11. **DODGE GERMS.** Use hand sanitizer on the plane to stave off sickness and saline nasal spray to avoid dryness.

12. **HIT THE GROUND RUNNING.** You need to stay up until it's bedtime in your destination to avoid prolonging your jet lag. A good way to do that is to go for a short run upon arrival.

13. **BE A FOLLOWER.** For meals before the prerace dinner, find places with a solid crowd of locals, indicating that the food is good and, more importantly, unlikely to make you sick.

14. **TAKE IT IN.** Once it's go time, remember that you came a long way to be on this starting line. Chat with other runners—the locals may give you tips for the rest of your trip—and consider the route a sightseeing tour. Bring a camera if you're so inclined, but make sure to stay out of the way of other runners when snapping shots or selfies.

TWENTY-THREE

STAYING INSPIRED

4 REASONS TO KEEP A RUNNING LOG[1]

Whether you do it digitally or on paper, keeping track of how far and fast you've run, and how you felt while doing it, is smart for a whole mess of reasons.

1. **IT KEEPS YOU ACCOUNTABLE.** You don't really want to see a big ugly gap in between otherwise successful blocks of training, do you? And in the event you *do* end up with a big ugly gap, a log helps you identify what was behind it. Were you overdoing it in the weeks leading up to the break? Did the gap coincide with a busy time at work? Learning your inconsistency triggers is the first step to solving them.
2. **YOU CAN IDENTIFY WHAT WORKS.** If you have an amazing race or a breakthrough workout, you can look back and see what you changed about your training to get that result.
3. **YOU CAN IDENTIFY WHAT CAUSES ILLNESS OR INJURY.** Perhaps you notice that exceeding a certain number of miles per week always leaves you with a nasty cold or aggravates

your hamstring, so you know you need to run fewer miles to stay healthy.

4. **IT CAN REINFORCE YOUR LOVE OF RUNNING.** Whether you have a truly great run once per week or once per year, those are the

> **BONUS TIP** If you struggle to keep a consistent routine, spend a month logging every run, *including* those you cut short or skip. This will help you pinpoint why you're so flaky, which can help you stop being that way.[2]

runs you *really* want to remember. "Nirvana runs" where you feel great enough to consider extending your run until forever are worth logging in great detail, so that on low-motivation days, you can look back and think, "Hey, maybe I'll feel *that* way if I head out today."[3]

HOW TO RESPOND TO 5 COMMON CRITIQUES FROM PEOPLE WHO DON'T RUN[4]

Nonrunners: They hate us 'cause they ain't us. (Or because they know a runner who never shuts up about his accomplishments, or because they still have nightmares about the gym class miles of their youth.) You'll eventually come across someone who enjoys nothing more than crapping on your pastime, so know how to keep your composure.

1. **"RUNNING WILL RUIN YOUR KNEES."** Studies show this simply isn't true—runners tend to have better bone and joint health than nonrunners. The more you use your body, the less likely you are to lose mobility, range of motion, and the ability to get around without pain or weakness.

2. **"RUNNING IS BORING."** It can be if you run the same routes, alone, every day, or if you primarily run on a treadmill. Exploring new places, running with different people, and doing a couple of harder or longer efforts each week adds variety and excitement. Music, audiobooks, and podcasts help a lot, too.

3. **"YOU SURE DON'T LOOK LIKE A RUNNER."** This one's just rude. You see all kinds of body types at the starting line of all kinds of race distances. How someone looks does not necessarily reflect how fit or healthy he or she is.

4. **"YOU'RE TOO SLOW TO CALL YOURSELF A RUNNER."** And this one's rude, too. Anyone who does any amount of running—even if it's slow, even if it includes walk breaks—is, by definition, a runner.

5. **"I WISH YOU'D STOP WASTING SO MUCH TIME ON RUNNING."** It's hard when loved ones don't encourage you. Sometimes, explaining what running does for you, physically and mentally, is enough to change minds. Other times, such as when running detracts from family time or keeps you from other responsibilities, you need to find a compromise.

6 REASONS TO BOTHER MEDITATING . . . [5]

Meditation: It's not just for monks. Many runners—both professional and amateur—have taken up the practice, and science says they're onto something. Here's how you can benefit.

1. **YOU'LL ENJOY RUNNING MORE.** Regular meditators report greater overall happiness and well-being, and they're better able to appreciate the delights of everyday life—like exercise.

2. **YOU'LL FEEL MORE ENERGIZED.** You know what wastes energy? The muscular tension that comes along with stress. Meditation reduces stress, which reduces tension, which reduces energy waste.

3. **YOU MAY DODGE INJURY.** Mindfulness meditation is all about tuning in to your body and your breath. That skill can help you notice and respond to aches and pains on the run before they become something more serious.

4. **YOU'LL UP YOUR TOLERANCE OF TOUGH RUNNING.** In meditation, you'll learn to notice sensations without judging them as "good" or "bad." When you're pushing the pace, you'll be better able to separate the sensation of your muscles and lungs working hard from the voice in your head that says, "Slow down!"

5. **YOU'LL BOOST ENDURANCE.** Long runs and races feel much more difficult when you fret over how much farther you have to go. Learn to stay in the moment and time will pass more quickly.

6. **YOU'LL STOP OBSESSING OVER YOUR GPS DEVICE.** A better connection with your breathing means a better sense of your effort level at any given time. You may rely less on your watch to know you're going the "right" speed once you're in touch with your natural sense of pace.

. . . AND 6 STEPS TO FOLLOW WHEN LEARNING HOW TO DO IT[6]

- Set a timer for 5 minutes. Start here and add a minute or so each time, ideally working up to 20 to 30 minutes. (But something is always better than nothing!)
- Sit or lie comfortably in a fairly quiet place with your eyes closed.
- Take a few deep breaths in and out through your nose, focusing on the air coming into your body and then leaving it.
- Continue to breathe deeply and slowly as you focus on your

body: Which areas seem tight? Which seem more relaxed? Notice how each part of you feels without judgment.

- Return your focus to your breath, breathing deeply and slowly.
- As thoughts enter your mind, notice them, then return to focusing on your breath. This will likely happen frequently, especially at first. Avoid judgment—even if your mind wanders, you're still benefiting from the session.

6 WAYS RUNNING CAN HELP YOU SOLVE PROBLEMS[7]

When you're hung up on a big problem, getting out for a run may not be high on your list of priorities. That said, it might be just what you need. Recent studies have found that the forward motion of running helps you be more forward-thinking, so you're better able to imagine the future and come up with creative solutions. Here's how to foster a eureka moment.

1. **SET THE STAGE.** As you get dressed to run or wait for your GPS to find satellites, spend 30 to 60 seconds thinking about the issue at hand.
2. **MAKE IT EASY.** Now's not the time to try a new route or a hard workout. You want your brain to be able to run more or less on autopilot. Instead of fretting over directions or whether you're hitting the right pace, you can devote your mental energy to your problem.
3. **TIME IT RIGHT.** You need to be awake and alert to be creative. While early morning runs are great when the purpose is to get your workout done, they may not be when the purpose is thinking outside the box.
4. **START WITH THE TOUGH STUFF . . .** If your problem is a particularly stressful one, focus on it early—you may feel more relaxed when you can attribute your rising heart rate to the act of running rather than to the crisis that's causing you stress.

5. **. . . . THEN LET IT SIT.** Too much ruminating on anxiety-inducing issues can lead to muscle tension and early fatigue. After a few minutes, focus on your breathing and your footfalls. An idea might break through once you're relaxed and present.

6. **TALK IT OUT.** When you're stuck on a problem, bringing in outside help might be the solution. Ask a friend you trust to go on an easy run with you, then spend some time explaining your situation. The idea-generating powers of a workout can help your friend be a better problem solver than he or she might be over a cup of coffee.

SECTION 5

169 TIPS FOR STAYING HEALTHY

THE 6 GOLDEN RULES OF INJURY PREVENTION[1]

1. **AVOID THE "TERRIBLE TOOS."** Doing too much, too fast, too soon is among the most common causes of injury. Increase mileage gradually, by no more than about 10 percent per week, have a solid base of comfortable miles before adding speed-work, and build in at least one easy or rest day between hard efforts (more if you're older or injury-prone). See "2 Rules to Help You Increase Mileage Safely" (page 6) for more specifics.

2. **WEAR THE RIGHT SHOES.** The wrong ones can cause an injury. Get fitted at a specialty store and replace shoes every 300 to 500 miles (or whenever they start feeling shot). "The 4 Golden Rules of Gear" (page 93) can tell you more about this.

3. **STRENGTH- AND CROSS-TRAIN.** Simple body-weight exercises can help correct muscular imbalances and weaknesses that lead to injury. Cardio cross-training (such as cycling, swimming, or sweatin' to the oldies with Richard Simmons) strengthens your heart and lungs and is less taxing on your bones and joints than running.

4. **LISTEN TO YOUR BODY.** If you have localized pain that's worse when you run, or any kind of discomfort that forces you to alter your gait, stop! Three to 7 days off from running may be enough to stop an issue from becoming a full-blown injury.[2]
5. **WARM UP AND COOL DOWN.** This is especially important whenever you'll be running harder than easy. The harder you'll be running, the more thorough your warmup ought to be. Start with 5 to 10 minutes of jogging and add strides (100-meter pickups) and dynamic stretches, like leg swings, skips, and high knees, before speedwork and short races.
6. **RECOVER FROM RACES.** The general rule is, each mile you race merits one easy run or rest day before you return to hard workouts. Wait 3 days after a 5K and 26 days after a full marathon.[3]

TWENTY-FOUR

MIDRUN ISSUES

---

4 SURFACES YOU CAN RUN ON (AND WHY YOU SHOULD SAMPLE THEM ALL)[1]

Though you might think running feels about the same no matter where you're doing it, your body feels otherwise. To be a well-rounded, less injury-prone runner, try at least one weekly run on a different surface than your usual go-to.

1. **ROADS AND SIDEWALKS.** Hard surfaces provide more bone-strengthening (and, sometimes, injury-causing) impact forces through your lower body. But if you're planning to race on roads, you should do a good amount of your training there—otherwise, be prepared to endure some extreme soreness during and after race day.

BONUS TIP No runner *has* to train on a treadmill (unless you've found some kind of futuristic treadmill race to enter). But if you use one, vary the incline between -1 percent and 3 percent to change up the stresses on your body and, if you're prepping for an outdoor event, you should plan to get on a racecourse-like surface at least weekly.

2. **TRAILS.** Smooth, crushed-gravel trails reduce impact forces without being too dissimilar to roads. Technical trails, which have rocks and roots, are also cushier, but because they challenge your stabilizing muscles and coordination, they pose a higher-than-usual risk of wipeout and ankle injury. To get the benefits without getting hurt, slow way down on tough terrain, and even walk through especially sketchy parts.

> **BONUS TIP** Logging too many miles on cambered roads—those where the shoulder is sloped to allow drainage—can anger your feet, legs, and hips. If you're injury-prone or increasing your mileage, move some or all of your miles to a level path, trail, or sidewalk.[2]

3. **TRACKS.** The surface is bouncy and flat, which is great for reaching top speed. Still, to run fast on rolling or hilly terrain, you'll need to do some speedy training there.

4. **GRASS.** With the exception of cross-country runners, not many people log miles on grass. If you have ankle problems, steer clear—grass covers up holes—but if you don't, end an occasional run with a few strides on grass to build stabilizing muscles.

> **BONUS TIP** Running intervals on the track can cause or exacerbate injuries due to the repetitive motion of turning left at a high rate of speed. If you have the track to yourself, try running about half your repeats in the opposite direction—so, clockwise instead of counterclockwise.[3]

4 WAYS TO PREVENT A MIDRUN CRAMP . . . [4]

When a muscle seems to take on a mind of its own—seizing and aching for no apparent reason—it can bring even a strong workout or race to a screeching halt. In fact, 39 percent of distance runners may experience cramps during competition. If you'd rather not be hobbling along just miles from the finish line, try these tactics.

1. **TRAIN PROPERLY.** One cramp-causing factor most experts can agree on is muscular fatigue. To prevent an issue on race day, put in the work in training, going long on a weekly basis. For a marathon, work up to at least a couple 20-milers. For shorter distances, it's best to exceed what you'll be doing on race day—getting up to 15 miles before a half marathon, for example.

2. **ADD PLYOMETRICS.** Explosive exercises like burpees, jump squats, and plyometric lunges may build endurance in your muscles' neurosensory receptors. The misfiring of these receptors may be what causes cramps.

3. **DON'T GO OUT TOO FAST.** Hammering the pace right out of the gate, especially if that pace is faster than what you trained to run, leads to muscular fatigue, and you already know that's bad.

4. **KNOW YOUR BODY.** Keep track of your midrun cramps and the variables surrounding them. Does it always happen after a certain number of miles? You may need to routinely run longer than that, at a slow pace, to adapt to the distance. Does it only happen when the temperature is above 70°F? You may need to take it easier in the heat. Once you can find a pattern, you can devise a customized solution. See "4 Reasons to Keep a Running Log" (page 145) if you're not convinced of their benefits.

. . . AND 2 WAYS TO GET A NASTY CRAMP TO GO AWAY[5]

1. **DRINKING PICKLE JUICE.** One researcher found that a double shot of pickle juice relieved cramps in an average of 85 seconds. If you

BONUS TIP Once you have a cramp, popular remedies that *won't* relieve it include consuming bananas, salt tablets, or mustard. Sorry!

think you can stomach it, try it.

2. **STRETCHING.** This is the most surefire way to find relief, but it usually requires you to stop running. Not ideal—but if you attempt to run through a cramp that changes your gait, you could hurt yourself.

> **BONUS TIP** Before a run is *not* the time to do static stretches (those you hold for 10-plus seconds). These stretches can detract from your muscles' explosive power, which slows you down and makes a run feel more difficult.[6] Instead, do dynamic moves like walking lunges, skips, and high knees, preferably after a jogging warmup.

3 NIPPLE PROBLEMS (AND HOW TO HANDLE THEM)

You might not think too much about your nipples (especially if you're a dude) until they're giving you all kinds of grief on a run. To keep your nipples out of sight and out of mind, here's how to solve some common issues.

1. **CHAFING.**[7] First of all, if you're wearing cotton shirts, switch to tech materials. If that doesn't help, try applying antichafing balm or plastic adhesive bandages before you start running. If you return from a run chafed, apply antichafing balm to affected areas before showering to reduce the sting. See "5 Weird (but Effective) Chafe-Stoppers" (page 110) for more ideas.

2. **BLEEDING.** This is a direct result of what happens when nipple chafing is

left unchecked. As soon as possible, rinse blood from your shirt with cold water and clean your nipples with soap and warm water. Cover them with plastic adhesive bandages on every run (or run shirtless) until they're healed.

3. **HEADLIGHTS.** If you're a woman who feels self-conscious during cold or wet runs, a thicker sports bra (or one with removable pads) can provide some extra coverage.

---

3 WAYS TO PROTECT YOURSELF FROM TICK BITES . . . [8]

Deer ticks are small—some are no larger than a freckle—but they can carry a mighty disease: Lyme. Its initial symptoms include fatigue, muscle weakness, and joint pain, and if it's not treated promptly, it can cause long-lasting problems like Bell's palsy, cognitive and cardiac issues, and chronic pain. Cases of Lyme have been reported in all 50 states, though it's most prevalent in the Northeast, mid-Atlantic, and Midwest. Take these preventive measures to avoid infection.

1. **REPEL BUGS.** Coat running clothes and shoes with permethrin, a repellent that lasts a month on your shoes and through 70 washings on your clothes. Keep treated apparel away from pets—it's especially toxic to cats.[9]
2. **STEER CLEAR OF FLORA.** Ticks are most often found in tall grasses, so if you're on a trail, stick to the center and avoid brushing up against plants. Consider wearing high socks treated with permethrin.
3. **CHECK YOURSELF.** After every run, do a thorough self-inspection. Although most ticks lie low, they can land on your lower body and crawl up. (Ew, right?) Search your underarms, head, groin, and waistline; around your ears; inside your belly button; and behind your knees. Remember, they're small, so look closely.

. . . AND 5 STEPS TO TAKE IF YOU GET ONE[10]

If you find a tick clinging to your skin, you're not doomed. Follow these instructions for best results.

1. **CAREFULLY REMOVE IT.** A tick must remain attached for 24 to 48 hours in order to transmit Lyme disease, so the sooner you can do this, the better. Use tweezers to grasp the tick as close to your skin as possible, pulling upward without twisting. The goal is to keep the body intact. Visit runnersworld.com/tickremoval for a video demonstration.

2. **KEEP IT.** Put the tick in a Ziploc bag and label it with the date and time of removal. This will come in handy if your doc wants to see it, or if you need to send it to a lab to test it for Lyme.

3. **CLEAN UP.** Disinfect the area the tick latched onto and wash your hands.

4. **ID IT.** Do some Googling to confirm that you're actually dealing with a tick that carries Lyme—only the blacklegged and western blacklegged varieties can. If you can't tell, assume the worst.

5. **CALL YOUR DOC.** If you removed the tick right after it latched on, you likely won't get infected, but if you're not sure how long it was there, your doc may recommend a preventive dose of antibiotics. If you start to experience symptoms—which take 2 weeks to appear—make an appointment ASAP.

TWENTY-FIVE

RECOVERY

THE 4 MOST IMPORTANT THINGS TO DO AFTER YOU RUN

---

1. **CHANGE.** Sitting or standing around in sweaty clothes can make you chilly, and chilly muscles don't recover as quickly as warm ones. Put on your comfiest sweatpants and coziest robe, then head to the kitchen to . . .

2. **. . . EAT AND DRINK.** You'll definitely want a glass of water, even after a short run. A hard or long run merits 150 to 300 calories of carbs and protein; find inspiration from "10 Totally Solid Postrun Recovery Snacks" (page 61). Grab a plate and roll out your yoga mat.

3. **STRETCH OR ROLL.** While there's some debate about the merits of static stretching, if it feels good, do it. Also do it if you have a limited range of motion on one side, since targeted stretching may help balance you and prevent injury.[1] Foam rolling tight or sore areas such as the IT bands,

> **BONUS TIP** Spending up to 10 minutes in the yoga pose legs up the wall can relieve tension in the legs, feet, and back after a hard run or workout.[2]

hamstrings, or quads can work out kinks.[3]

4. **LOG.** While the details of your run are fresh in your mind, write them down. In addition to mileage and pace, you may want to track which shoes you were wearing, which route you ran, and how you felt. Now hit the shower—you stink!

> **BONUS TIP** Make the most of Netflix binges by foam rolling while you watch.[4] Target your calves, IT bands, glutes, hamstrings, adductors, and quads.[5] Roll each area for 30 to 90 seconds at a time, up to three times in one session, and limit your total roller time to no more than 20 minutes per day.[6]

4 WAYS TO MAKE THE MOST OF YOUR POST-LONG-RUN ICE BATH

As if distance running weren't masochistic enough, some half and full marathoners swear by submerging their bottom halves in a tub filled with ice water after their longest training runs. There's debate over whether this is wise. While studies show that ice baths do reduce inflammation, you may reap more benefits from a session if you let your body work through that inflammation on its own.[7] If you hate ice baths, skip them. If you need to recover quickly—between relay legs, say, or if you're running two races in one weekend—here's how to ice-bathe right.

1. **NAIL THE TIME AND TEMPERATURE.** Spend 10 to 20 minutes in water that's between 50° and 59°F and deep enough to submerge your legs.[8] Don't worry too much about exact temp. Cold water with a few trays of ice cubes should suffice.

2. **KEEP YOUR UPPER BODY WARM.** Break out your upper-body winter running garb and wear a hat and a couple warm layers on your torso you can roll up to keep out of the water.[9]

3. **HAVE A HOT BEVERAGE.** Tea, coffee, cocoa: All will make you feel less miserable.

4. EMBRACE PRINT. Reading a paper copy of *Runner's World* is a much safer option than taking your smartphone or tablet into the tub. Just sayin'.

BONUS TIP Reducing your mileage by about 15 to 20 percent every 3 weeks—taking a "stepback" or "down" week—can promote recovery, which helps you crush the following week's workouts.[10]

3 WAYS YOUR BRAIN CAN HELP YOUR BODY RECOVER FASTER[11]

Challenging exercise stimulates the release of the stress hormone cortisol as well as an inflammatory response in fatigued muscles, so feeling "blah" after hard or long workouts is what's supposed to happen. But compression gear, foam roller sessions, and other physical interventions aren't the only ways to bounce back. These mental techniques create similar physical changes—use them in addition to traditional recovery methods to go from "blah" to "ahhh" in record time.

1. **HANG IN NATURE.** Science shows that feelings of awe (such as what you might feel when taking in a panoramic view at sunrise) are linked to lower inflammatory markers. The day

after a hard effort, go for a recovery walk or jog somewhere awe-inspiring and ditch your phone and earbuds. The more you marvel, the better you'll feel.

2. **HANG WITH FRIENDS.** Physiological markers of stress return to baseline faster when you spend time with other runners after a hard workout or race than when you spend time solo. It's a great reason to make post-long-run brunch with buddies a regular thing.

3. **THINK POSITIVE.** End each training-log entry with something that went well that day, even if it's only "I got out to run when I didn't really want to." Research shows that positive reflections postrun generate a hormonal response that promotes recovery. You can still critique yourself—just save it for the next day, after your body has had a chance to rebuild.

5 SLEEP RULES FOR RUNNERS[12]

If your motto is "I'll sleep when I'm dead," choose a new motto. Seven to 9 hours of shut-eye per night is the baseline for most adults, and runners may need more. Sleeping too little inhibits muscle and bone recovery, limits the gains you make from hard training, suppresses your immune system, and generally wreaks havoc on your health and fitness. Make the most of your sleep by following these guidelines.

1. **DISCOVER HOW MUCH YOU NEED.** A weeklong vacation, sans alarm, is a good opportunity to learn your perfect sleep schedule. You'll spend the first few days catching up on your sleep debt. The average amount you sleep on nights four onward is about what you need on any given night.

2. **TRACK IT.** Log your sleep time and quality alongside your mileage to see patterns in how snoozing affects your performance and overall well-being. Make it your goal to log your perfect amount more nights than not.

3. **PRACTICE GOOD "SLEEP HYGIENE."** This means going to

bed and waking up at about the same time each day, avoiding screens and bright lights for 30 minutes to an hour before you plan to hit the hay, and keeping your bedroom dark and cool.[13]

4. **SLEEP IN.** If you're setting your alarm for a time less than 6 hours in the future to squeeze in a run, maybe reconsider: You benefit more from an extra hour of sleep than you would from the half-assed workout you'll do when sleep-deprived. (Research shows athletes can perform as well after a night of no sleep as they do on a good night's sleep, but the same effort feels considerably harder.) If you can do the workout later in the day, do that.

5. **BE REALISTIC.** Sometimes life makes it so you can't get your perfect amount of sleep. (Hello new parents, med students, and anyone whose job involves a "busy season.") You can certainly train through the chaos, but save the PR-chasing for calmer times.

6 WAYS TO GET A BETTER NIGHT OF SLEEP BEFORE A WORKOUT OR RACE[14]

Robots have it good: Flip a switch to "off," and they power down. If only humans were able to sleep on command! Unfortunately, when we most desperately *want* to rest—like the night before a hard effort—sleep proves the most elusive. The key is to be prepared for the next day . . . and then to forget about what's to come as much as possible. Here are some strategies borrowed from elite runners to ensure you rest your best.

1. **CHECK THE FORECAST.** If you need to adjust the timing or location of your morning run due to thunderstorms, high winds, ice, or other potentially dangerous conditions, it's best to know the night before. You can't adjust the timing of a race, but you *can* make sure you're dressed appropriately for the weather. If it'll be storming when you planned to run and you can move it earlier, do so, or else plan to hit the treadmill.

2. **SET UP YOUR COFFEEMAKER.** Why bother getting out of bed at all if coffee isn't in your immediate future? Reduce the lag time between waking up and enjoying your morning cup of java by grinding the beans and pouring in the water the night before. Better yet, set a programmable maker so the pot's ready just as your alarm is sounding.

3. **LAY OUT YOUR CLOTHES . . .** Don't forget your watch, sunglasses, and whatever other accessories you may choose (and your bib and timing chip, if you're racing). The less stumbling around and searching you need to do while half asleep, the better.

4. **. . . OR PUT THEM ON.** If you're just running in shorts and a tee, you might as well sleep in them. As long as it's comfortable, that's one less morning step!

5. **SHUT OFF YOUR BRAIN.** Once you have everything prepped, it's time to stop running around and thinking about the next day. Shift your focus to something that doesn't require a lot of focus: reruns of your favorite sitcom, a book that's not mentally taxing or scary, or a simple board game with your family or friends.

6. **TAKE A FEW DEEP, CALMING BREATHS.** Once you're in bed, spend a few minutes taking deep belly breaths, focusing on the air flowing into your torso as your stomach rises, then the air flowing out as your stomach contracts.

TWENTY-SIX

STRENGTH AND CROSS-TRAINING

---

4 OPPORTUNITIES TO MOVE MORE[1]

The phrase "sitting is the new smoking" isn't entirely accurate. For one, sitting doesn't coat your lungs with black gunk. For another, sitting itself isn't the issue: It's remaining in a single stationary position for long periods of time. (Parking in chairs just happens to be our favorite fixed position, and runners do it as much as sedentary folks—about 9 hours each day.) For better health and better range of motion, try moving more . . .

1. . . . **AT WORK.** Take 2- to 3-minute breaks every half hour to stand, stretch, or walk around the office. Drinking lots of water will not only ensure that you're hydrated—it'll also force you to stand every hour or two for bathroom breaks.
2. . . . **DURING BREAKS.** Walk, whether around the building, outside the building, or simply to grab lunch or coffee. If you find yourself waiting in line, shift your weight from one foot to the other, dropping your hip on the side that's planted to raise your other foot off the ground.
3. . . . **AFTER LONG RUNS.** Recover, but don't lie around all day—a 20- to 30-minute nap should be the most you need. If you're going to be watching TV or reading, sit on the floor and

cycle through various positions (cross-legged, feet sole-to-sole, legs out in a V) every half hour or so.

4. . . . **ON REST DAYS.** "Rest" doesn't mean "be a total slug." Walk or bike to run errands. Garden on your hands and knees. Play with your kids. Stay in motion however you can. Your next run will be better for it.

A 5-MOVE, NO-FRILLS STRENGTH-TRAINING PLAN[2]

If you love pumping iron, you probably already know infinity strength-training moves and how they help your running. If you'd rather just run, know that you'll be more likely to do so without injury if you do some basic strength work. This routine by Chicago-based running coach Jenny Hadfield is the bare minimum. You only need to do each move for 1 minute after two or three runs per week.

1. **PLANK.** Rise up on your forearms and toes so your body forms a straight line from head to foot and hold. If this is too tough, drop to your knees for some or all of the minute.

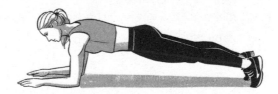

2. **PUSHUPS.** With your hands and toes on the floor and your body in a straight line, lower yourself, keeping your elbows close to your sides, push back up, and repeat. If this is too tough, rest on your knees instead of your toes.

3. **LEG CURLS.** On your back, with feet hip-width apart on a stability ball, raise your hips. Pull the ball toward you, push it away from you, and repeat.

4. **LUNGES.** Stand with feet hip-width apart. Step forward with your right leg, lower until your left knee is close to the floor, then push up through your right heel back to standing. Switch legs and continue alternating.

5. **SQUATS.** Stand with feet hip-width apart. Lower your butt, pushing your hips back and down. Push through your heels to stand, then repeat.

---

5 WAYS TO STICK TO A STRENGTH-TRAINING ROUTINE[3]

You know you have to do it—especially if you've been injured in the past—but who wants to be stuck inside a gym when you *could* be outside running, feeling footloose and fancy-free? If fear of injury isn't enough incentive, try these tricks.

1. **PICK SIX . . .** You only need a handful of moves if injury prevention is your goal, so choose two for each bodily region (upper body, core, lower body). They don't have to be complicated; body-weight moves (such as clamshells, leg lifts, bridges, and planks) are adequate.

2. **. . . AND THEN PICK SIX MORE.** It's best to change up your routine as your body adapts (about once a month). If you don't feel like selecting new exercises, you can simply do more reps or add weight to make your go-tos more challenging.

3. **SCHEDULE IT . . .** If you're good about sticking to a training plan, put strength training *on* the plan. Schedule a short

postrun session two or three times per week. Experts disagree about whether it's better to strength train after hard runs or easy runs, so just choose what you're more likely to do and then save rest days for total rest.

4. **. . . OR TRY "SNACKS."** If the only thing you want to do postrun is shower, plot short strength bursts throughout your day: a plank after rolling out of bed, a series of lunges on your way out the door, a wall-sit right after you return home.

5. **TAKE A CLASS.** Finding one you love can take the angst out of strength training, and paying for the privilege makes you more likely to show up. Just remember that intense ones like boot camp or CrossFit might detract from your running, so save those for your off-season.

3 RUNNING WORKOUTS THAT TEACH YOU TO ENGAGE YOUR GLUTES

Your buns are good for more than just sitting: You're also less likely to get hurt if your rear is strong and engaged. While strengthening your backside in the gym with moves like squats and lunges can help, you also need to train those muscles to activate while you run.[4] Try one of these workouts each week.

1. **BELTLINE TEST.**[5] While running on a treadmill in front of a mirror, watch your beltline. If it visibly dips to one side, your glutes aren't engaging properly. Simply continuing to run while trying to keep your hips level helps fire up those muscles.

2. **HILL SPRINTS.** After a mile or two of warmup jogging, find a fairly steep hill (up to 10 percent grade) and do six to ten 10- to 20-second sprints uphill, recovering fully with 90 seconds of walking between reps.[6] Cool down for a mile or two.

3. **LONG, STEADY HILLS.** If you have a long climb of a few miles or more available to you, as well as someone who can pick you up at the top, you'll engage your muscles in a similar

way to hill sprints.[7] However, these runs are more taxing, so save them for after you've mastered sprints.

5 REASONS TO DO YOGA . . . [8]

Yoga has more going for it than just the comfy pants.

1. **YOU'LL BUILD FLEXIBILITY.** This one's kind of obvious, but your goal isn't to look like the bendy model in a Lululemon catalog. Yoga can mitigate excessive tightness that affects your gait or range of motion and increases injury risk, especially if it's more pronounced on one side of your body.

2. **YOU'LL BREATHE BETTER.** In yoga, you learn to breathe from your diaphragm, which oxygenates your blood better than shallow breaths. Carry that over to running for an extra boost with every inhalation.

3. **YOU'LL TRAIN YOUR BRAIN.** The ability to remain present and avoid dwelling on discomfort can help you avoid panicking or tensing up when a run gets tough.

4. **YOU'LL LEARN ABOUT YOUR BODY.** Doing every pose on both sides helps you reveal potential injury-causing imbalances in strength or flexibility you might not have noticed while running.

5. **YOU'LL GET STRONG ALL OVER.** Yoga requires upper-body strength that running does not. Additionally, poses that require balance strengthen hip and core muscles that protect the lower body from misalignment and injury.

. . . AND 4 WAYS TO WORK IT INTO YOUR SCHEDULE[9]

1. **START SLOWLY.** If you're a total noob, begin by trying out a few key poses like pigeon (pictured at right), revolved low lunge, and legs up the wall at home. Supplement with a

5-minute meditation to build focus and mindfulness—several apps offer guided options.

2. **SAMPLE THE OFFERINGS.** You can take an in-person class— if you're just starting out, choose one marked for beginners—or try one of the many routines offered online. (We have some at runnersworld.com/yogacenter.) If you don't love a style or instructor, keep searching until you find your match.

3. **CHILL OUT.** Yoga isn't a race, so don't try to compete with your classmates. Focus on what you're doing and ignore everyone else—except the instructor, who can ensure you're doing the poses correctly. When in doubt, opt for a shallower stretch—you don't want to hurt yourself.

4. **AVOID OVERDOING IT.** You can do restorative yoga pretty much whenever you want, but avoid power or advanced varieties the day before a hard or long running workout or race.

---

4 RUNNER-FRIENDLY WAYS TO BUILD FITNESS WITHOUT ADDING MILES[10]

Every one of us has an upper limit on how much running we can handle before we get hurt—and far too many of us have discovered that limit the hard way. Once you know your limit, though, you can still train more if you choose a low-impact activity. Even if you've never been hurt, cross-training activities like these make you a more well-rounded, injury-resistant athlete.

1. **POOL RUNNING.** This is the best option for long-distance PR seekers who are maxing out their miles on land. The motion of jogging in the deep end with a flotation belt on closely mimics running, and you can do an intense cardiovascular workout without feeling it in your muscles and joints the next day. Go for 45 to 60 minutes, and make the time pass faster by throwing in some 15- to 30-second "sprints" and 5- to 10-minute tempo-effort phases between bouts of recovery.

2. **WEIGHT TRAINING.** Building strength helps build speed. One study found that lifting heavy weights improved 5K finishing times better than lifting light weights. Ease into it, starting with weights that will allow you to do about 12 reps per set. Then add weight and decrease reps—you'll want it to be challenging to complete six. Visit runnersworld.com /strengthtraining for a multitude of routines to try.

3. **ROWING.** If you tend to become more and more wilted as a race goes on, the indoor rowing machine is for you. You won't only work your legs—you'll shore up your arms, back, and core, the muscles that keep you upright even as you fatigue. Try doing three 10-minute interval sets: 8 minutes alternating 20 seconds hard and 10 seconds easy, followed by 2 minutes recovery.

4. **CYCLING.** Riding requires you to engage your quads, hamstrings, and glutes—your hill-climbin' muscles. Bike workouts will help you charge up inclines on the run. You can simply find a rolling course to ride outdoors, or you can take a spin class that encourages you to ratchet up resistance—while sitting and standing—to simulate hills.

TWENTY-SEVEN

INJURIES

HOW TO IDENTIFY THE 7 MOST COMMON RUNNING INJURIES . . . [1]

It's hard to quantify how many runners get hurt every year. Studies suggest the number is somewhere between 19 and 79 percent—not helpful.[2] If you fear you may be joining that indefinitely sized group, check your symptoms here.

1. **RUNNER'S KNEE.** Pain on the inside or outside of the knee that you experience during or after runs, when you stand after sitting for a while, or as you descend a hill or a flight of stairs. If you've got it really bad, it'll even bother you when you walk.

2. **ACHILLES TENDINITIS.** Pain in the area just above your heel, where it connects to your ankle, during a run, after a run, or when standing on your toes. You may also experience swelling.

3. **HAMSTRING PROBLEMS.** Achiness, tightness, or pain in the muscle that runs between your butt and the back of your knee that may be more pronounced while climbing hills or running fast. You may find some relief by slowing down or taking shorter steps. Severe problems, like a pull, will involve a sharp pain that comes on suddenly, possibly with bruising afterward.

4. **PLANTAR FASCIITIS.** This feels like an ache or a bruise along your arch or on your heel that's often at its worst first thing in the morning, when you stand after extended sitting, or in the beginning of a run. Severe cases hurt all the time.

5. **SHIN SPLINTS.** Tightness and aching along the shins while running. If it hurts when you're not running or when you hop on the affected leg, it could be a serious case—or worse, a stress reaction or fracture.

6. **ILIOTIBIAL BAND SYNDROME (ITBS).** Pain along the outside of your leg, possibly near the knee, that flares up after about 10 minutes of running but is relieved by walking. If you've got it bad, you may experience pain on the outside of the leg when walking down a hill or a flight of stairs.

7. **STRESS FRACTURES.** These can occur in a variety of locations, but they're most commonly found in the feet, shins, and heels. If you're experiencing localized, acute pain all the time—pain that gets progressively worse if you try to run—get thee to a doctor for an X-ray ASAP.

. . . AND HOW TO TREAT THEM IF THEY HAPPEN TO YOU[3, 4]

If you're hurt enough to have to stop or drastically limit your running, it suddenly feels like everyone and their mom is outside logging frequent, wonderful miles and taking that privilege for granted. (Jerks!) Here's how to limit the time you spend being that bitter, injured person.

1. **RUNNER'S KNEE.** Reduce your mileage and take extra rest days. It may be less painful to run uphill, so hit the treadmill and set it to a gentle incline. To strengthen your quads, which hold the kneecap in alignment, set a slow walking pace on the 'mill, bump the incline to 5 percent, and walk backward while holding the handrails. (Looking like a weirdo is the price you pay to get healthy.) Lateral side steps (also known as monster walks)

strengthen weak hips and glutes. Loop a resistance band around your ankles, bend your knees slightly, and take 10 to 15 small steps to the right, then to the left, and repeat twice more.

2. **ACHILLES TENDINITIS.** Take a few days off and focus on icing the area at least five times each day. (It's a lot, but you want to heal, right?) You can cross-train, but avoid cycling, which can worsen the problem. Once the tendon feels better, strengthen the area with heel drops: Stand on a step with your heels hanging off and use your calves to lower and raise your heels 20 times.

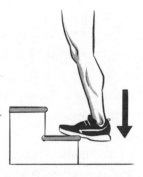

3. **HAMSTRING PROBLEMS.** Pulls require a long layoff—that means weeks to months. You can cycle, pool run, and swim to

stay fit as long as they don't aggravate the injury. If your injury is less severe, you may be able to run slowly on flat ground without pain. Do bridge walkouts to build strength and flexibility: Lie on your back, raise your hips, and walk your feet away from your butt, alternating right- and left-side steps.

4. **PLANTAR FASCIITIS.** If it's really bad, you may need 3 months to a year (!) off from running. (Take time off sooner rather than later to shorten the recovery period.) In the meantime, pool running and swimming are safe bets, and you may cycle or use an elliptical machine if you can do so without pain. Freeze a cylindrical water bottle and roll your foot on it several times a day to relieve discomfort. Strengthen your calves (see "Achilles tendinitis," above, to learn about heel drops) and avoid walking around barefoot or in shoes without proper support.

5. **SHIN SPLINTS.** Back off on running, although cycling, pool running, and swimming are all okay. Assess your footwear: Are your running shoes old? Replace them. Have they never felt quite right? Hit the local specialty store to get fitted for another pair—runners with very high or low arches are more prone to this issue. Wearing an ankle brace while running as you recover can take some stress off your shin muscles, as can taking shorter, more frequent steps.

6. **ILIOTIBIAL BAND SYNDROME (ITBS).** Take a few rest days and get cozy with your foam roller—rolling the outside of your leg between your knee and your hip can help relieve pain. Swimming is pretty much the only cardio activity you can do that won't irritate the IT band. Do lateral side steps to

strengthen key areas. When you return to running, roll before and after you run, and adopt a slightly wider stance than you usually would to reduce friction. Avoid hills until you can run on level ground without pain.

> **BONUS TIP** If you're chronically injured, try taking shorter, quicker steps. This may reduce the impact force your body absorbs with each stride, which keeps your bones, joints, and muscles from becoming as cranky.[5]

7. **STRESS FRACTURE.** You're in for some serious time off: You'll need 8 to 16 weeks to recover. You may pool run and swim because they're no-impact. Any kind of strength training can help improve your bone density—as can ensuring you're getting enough calories and nutrients in your diet—but follow the instructions your doctor gives you.

---

5 WAYS YOUR BODY CAN TELL YOU, "HELP! ENOUGH!"[6]

If you've heard the term "overtraining," you may think it's something that only happens to professional runners who log more miles in a week than you do in a month. Not so. Your body and mind can only handle so much stress, from running or otherwise, so during a chaotic time it'll take fewer miles to burn you out.[7] Watch out for these red flags.

1. **AN ELEVATED RESTING HEART RATE.** If you track your pulse daily, and it's higher than usual, this is a physiological indicator that you could use a day (or a few) off.
2. **FATIGUE.** Feeling run-down even after a few nights of seemingly solid sleep is not normal. Plus, overtraining can *cause* insomnia or poor-quality sleep—either way, you need rest.
3. **ILLNESS.** Overdoing it taxes your immune system. Take it easy until you're feeling better.
4. **POOR PERFORMANCE.** If you have a streak of runs that feel

harder than you think they should, that's your body saying, "Seriously, give me a break."

5. **CRANKINESS.** Research shows your mood is an even better indicator of overtraining than objective measures like resting heart rate.[8] Add a simple mood-tracking rubric to your log: Try a happy face for "felt good," a sad face for "felt bad," and a neutral face for "meh." If you see too many "bads" and "mehs," take a few days to regroup.

3 TYPES OF FOOTWEAR THAT CAN CAUSE INJURIES (OR MAKE EXISTING ONES WORSE)

If only we lived in a world in which comfort was king, in which pants with stretchy waistbands and orthopedic shoes were considered the highest fashion. Alas, we do not. But it's still helpful to know which nonrunning shoes might be creating the issues you feel on your runs.

1. **HIGH HEELS.** Heels force your weight onto the balls of your feet and shorten your calves.[9] If you must wear heels, stretch your calves regularly and find ones with a cushioned forefoot.[10] If you have problems with your Achilles tendons, which connect your calf muscles to your heel bones, you should avoid heels altogether.[11]

2. **FLATS.** These workplace-appropriate alternatives to heels often do not absorb shock well, which can lead to heel or forefoot pain.[12] The flim-

BONUS TIP If you're going to be doing a lot of standing or walking, but still need to wear one of these three types of footwear at some point, wear supportive, well-cushioned shoes when you can get away with it. Tote along the other shoes and slip them on only when you need to. For example, if you're a woman in a wedding party, wear heels for the staged photos and switch to low, supportive shoes for dancing at the reception.

sier the flat, the worse they are for your feet.

3. **FLIP-FLOPS.**[13] These aren't supportive either, and having to use your toes to keep them from flopping off can cause problems with your Achilles tendons. Sandals with arch support and straps that secure behind your heels are a better bet.

> **BONUS TIP** If you're looking to re-create the opening scene from *Chariots of Fire* on your next vacation, take care: Barefoot running (even on sand) can leave you sore or injured. If you must hit the beach, wear shoes, socks, and antichafing balm on your feet, and run an out-and-back route on the hard-packed sand near the water.[14]

5 FORM CUES TO PREVENT TREADMILL-INDUCED INJURIES[15]

Training on the treadmill beats not training at all, but it isn't the same as outdoor running. Roads and trails are stationary beneath you, and you can slow down or stop without needing to fiddle with buttons first. To run on this contraption, you must pay more attention to *how* you're running than you might in a more natural setting.

1. **MOVE YOUR ARMS.** The handrails aren't meant to be clung to. They can be helpful when you're mounting, dismounting, or changing speeds, but for the most part, move your arms as you would outdoors to prevent pain in and below your knees.

2. **KEEP A LEVEL GAZE.** Looking down at the display—or askance, at a TV that's not directly in front of you—can create tension in the neck and shoulders. Plus, it's harder to stay on a belt when you're not looking straight ahead.

3. **AVOID OVERSTRIDING.** Replicate the stride rate you maintain outdoors. Count every footfall on one side—at easy paces *and* during speedwork—on the treadmill and on the roads or track to compare. Taking fewer steps on the treadmill likely

means you're overstriding to keep up with the fast-moving belt, and that can cause a litany of injuries.

4. **AVOID A TOO-NARROW STANCE . . .** The fear that you'll step on the sides instead of the moving belt can produce an unnaturally narrow stance. You want the insides of your feet to approach but not cross over an imaginary line drawn from your belly button to the ground.

5. **. . . AND A TOO-NARROW ARM SWING.** You don't want your arms to cross the centerline of your body, either, but you may be more likely to move your arms this way if you're concerned about hitting the rails. You should be far enough back from the front of the belt that this isn't an issue.

3 REASONS TO SAY NO TO DRUGS[16]

It's tempting to pop a pill for every ache and pain, especially when over-the-counter anti-inflammatories are marketed as harmless, but resist! Here's what happens when you abstain.

1. **YOU'LL RECOVER BETTER.** The body's natural inflammatory process exists for a reason. It helps damaged tissue build back stronger after a tough workout. Taking something can interfere with that process.

2. **YOU MAY DODGE INJURY.** Masking your body's cries for help and running when you should be resting can lead to the development, or worsening, of a serious problem.

3. **YOU'LL BE LESS LIKELY TO GET SICK.** Anti-inflammatory drugs decrease antibody production, per a 2009 study. Because hard training on its own messes with immunity, adding drugs to the equation makes you more vulnerable to bugs.

6 STRATEGIES TO SPEED YOUR RETURN FROM INJURY[17]

A runner who never gets hurt is like a unicorn: magical, mystical, and fictional. Log enough miles and you'll almost certainly end up with some kind of issue, whether it's a twisted ankle from a tumble on a trail or a cranky knee caused by doing more than your body can handle. Here's how to cope when it happens to you.

1. **KEEP MOVING.** Good news: Sometimes you can run through an injury—*if* slowing way down allows you to run without pain. If running hurts no matter what, though, you'll change your gait to make it hurt less, which can lead to another injury. In those cases, maintain fitness with a low- to no-impact cardio activity like biking, swimming, or pool running.

2. **ROLL AND STRETCH.** To boost healing blood flow, foam-roll religiously, before and after each workout. Dynamic stretches help, too. Skip any moves that aggravate your injury (duh).

3. **ADJUST YOUR DIET.** Running torches calories like few other activities can. (But you knew that!) So when you're running less or not at all, limit calorie-dense indulgences like pizza, beer, and ice cream and include protein, which helps repair injured muscles, in every meal. Eggs, fish, and beans are all good sources.

4. **LIMIT ALCOHOL.** Boozing in the 2-day window postinjury can contribute to swelling and slow down recovery, so just don't, okay? After that, keep it moderate—no more than a drink or two per day.

5. **MEDICATE *SOMETIMES*.** Research suggests that popping anti-inflammatories like ibuprofen may interfere with the healing process. But if the pain's keeping you up at night, take something. Sleep is critical to muscle repair, so do everything you can to get enough.

6. **STAY CALM.** If logging miles is your stress relief, you'll need to find another way to manage—especially if not running is causing more stress. Other forms of cardio can help, as can yoga and meditation. A 2015 study found that walking in nature quashed negative thoughts more effectively than a walk in an urban area, so if you're able to, head somewhere scenic to do it.

A few planned weeks without running each year can prevent burnout, but a few *unplanned* weeks off can sap your fitness and increase your risk of injury when you return. You can get your old running self back—it'll just take some time and caution. Here's how to do it, depending on why you've been out.

1. **YOU WERE INJURED.** You have to be very careful to avoid reinjuring whatever was bothering you. Start by run-walking for 20 to 30 minutes every other day. The walk breaks will reduce some of the impact on your body. Progress, slowly, toward your previous weekly volume, keeping every run easy and using pain as your guide—if anything hurts, back off. Once you're running the number of miles you were before sans pain, you can gradually add in speedwork and tempo runs.

2. **YOU'VE BEEN BUSY.** If you've got a new job or child that's taking up a lot of your time, you'll need to schedule in runs when you can. Block out some time whenever you're least busy—for most, that's early in the morning—and start with short, easy-paced runs. Don't be too hard on yourself: If you're not getting a lot of sleep, you might be better off changing the time or reducing the frequency of your runs to log more ZZZs. Just 30 minutes of running three or four times per week is enough to maintain fitness, so aim for that.

3. **YOU'VE PUT ON SOME POUNDS.** Extra weight will slow you down, but don't dwell on it. Try running for time instead of distance on soft surfaces, which will reduce the impact on your bones and joints, and also include no-impact cardio cross-training such as cycling, swimming, or using the elliptical on nonrunning days. Two or three times per week, work in some strength training, as research shows that cardio plus weights burns more fat than cardio alone.

4. **YOU JUST DIDN'T FEEL LIKE RUNNING.** Make a change or

find a cause to revive your love of running. Plan a "race-cation," register for a distance that's new to you, or run for a charity that's dear to your heart. Sometimes, running for others can be more motivating than doing it for yourself.

5. **YOU TOOK MORE TIME OFF POSTRACE THAN YOU INTENDED.** Taking a break postrace is smart, but limit it to a few weeks. Then work back toward your previous volume, doing speed and tempo runs only if you want to, and avoid signing up for another race until you really feel you can commit to the training.

COMEBACK-MILEAGE GUIDELINES FOR 4 LEVELS OF LAYOFFS

How long you were out determines the percentage of your former weekly mileage you can safely handle upon your return. Follow these rules *unless* you were injured—in that case, you'll need to be even more conservative.

1.	8 to 15 days	75 to 90 percent
2.	2 to 3 weeks	60 to 75 percent
3.	4 weeks to a month	50 to 60 percent
4.	More than a month	40 to 50 percent

TWENTY-EIGHT

ILLNESS

THE 4 RULES OF RUNNING (OR RESTING) WHILE SICK . . . [1]

If you're feeling under the weather and wondering, "Can I still do my workout?" you're either not *that* sick (yet) or you're a stubborn, type-A runner. Here's your cheat sheet for the next cold and flu season.

1. **START WITH THE "NECK RULE" . . .** Symptoms above the neck, like sneezing or a runny nose, are usually safe to run through, while any below the neck, like achiness or chest congestion, require rest days.
2. **. . . BUT KNOW ITS EXCEPTION.** If you have a sinus infection, which includes the aforementioned above-the-neck symptoms *plus* headache and sinus pressure, you need to rest for at least 3 days. If you try to train through a sinus infection, it can escalate into pneumonia.
3. **CONSIDER TRAINING INDOORS.** If you're prone to sinus infections, dry, cold winter air can cause a flare-up. Try treadmill or pool running some days to avoid getting sick, or when you're coming back after an infection.

4. **WAIT OUT A FEVER.** If you have a temperature above 99°F, do not exercise. Wait until you've been fever-free for at least 24 hours, then try a short, easy run. Wait at least a week or two before increasing your volume and intensity to where it was before your illness.

. . . AND 3 NOT-OBVIOUS STRATEGIES TO AVOID GETTING SICK IN THE FIRST PLACE[2]

Hopefully, you already know that eating well, washing your hands regularly, and getting enough sleep can help you avoid coming down with something nasty. You might not already know to do these things.

1. **SCHEDULE FLIGHTS CAREFULLY.** If you must travel on those germ boxes in the sky, at least consider the timing: A 2016 study found that athletes were five times likelier to report symptoms of illness the day after flying than usual and three times likelier the day after a race. Avoid if at all possible the double whammy of flying immediately after a race or hard workout, and take an easy or rest day upon returning home.
2. **FUEL AND REFUEL.** Carbs during and after a long run can help tamp down the inflammatory response that causes weakened immunity after long efforts. Take some in midrun when you'll be out longer than 75 to 90 minutes, and take in more with protein ASAP postrun.
3. **GET ENOUGH D.** Vitamin D supports the immune system, and you may not be getting enough—especially during winter, when there's less sunlight. It's hard to get enough through diet (though fortified milk, fatty fish, and eggs are good sources), so talk to your doc about a supplement.

5 WAYS TO COMBAT ALTITUDE SICKNESS[3]

If you live at or near sea level, do some research before booking your next big trip: You might develop mondo headaches while visiting destinations at elevations of 6,000 feet or higher, and because of the lower levels of oxygen in the air, you'll likely have trouble working out there, too. This doesn't mean that running meccas such as Flagstaff, Arizona (7,000 feet),[4] and Mammoth Lakes, California (7,800 feet),[5] are forever off-limits to you—if you're prepared.

1. **EASE IN.** If possible, spend one night at a destination with an in-between elevation before going up high. For example, stay a night in Denver, Colorado (5,280 feet), before heading to Vail (8,120 feet). Try to arrive at the highest elevation at least 3 to 5 days before you plan to race there, but 7 to 14 days is better, if you can swing it.

2. **SHAKE IT OUT.** Upon arriving at altitude, do a 30-minute, conversational run to observe how altitude affects you.

3. **LEARN TO BREATHE.** At altitude, you might feel short of breath—and even more so when you're *running* at altitude. Start by relaxing your jaw, which is likely among the places that are tense as you huff and puff, and breathe out with a "sss" or "thhh" sound to relax your vocal cords.

4. **HYDRATE.** You'll need about a liter more of water per day at altitude than you need at home. When in doubt, check your pee—it should be pale yellow. Darker means you're dehydrated; lighter means you're overdoing it, which can also be dangerous.

5. **LOWER YOUR EXPECTATIONS.** An easy effort at altitude will produce slower paces than the same effort at sea level. Race paces are similarly affected. You *will* run more slowly than you're used to at altitude—get over it, or leave your watch in the hotel and run by feel.

5 THINGS RUNNERS NEED TO KNOW ABOUT BLOOD CLOTS[6]

Known risk factors for blood clots include being sedentary and smoking—things that most athletes just don't do. That said, runners aren't immune to clots, and there are some times we might be at especially high risk. Remember these facts.

1. **THE CAUSES.** In athletes, clots can happen due to dehydration (the blood is more viscous), acute injury (the venous walls are damaged from a muscle strain), or low blood pressure coupled with periods of inactivity (the blood pools in your feet and legs). Clotting disorders can contribute as well, and you may not know if you have one.

2. **WHEN TO BE ON HIGH ALERT.** Long trips, especially on airplanes, can promote pooling and clots. Your risk is even higher if you're traveling after a race, when you may be dehydrated *and* have muscle damage.

3. **HOW TO PREVENT CLOTS.** Stay hydrated—your urine should be pale yellow at all times. Stand and move around as much as possible on long flights or car rides and keep your legs moving while you're seated. Circle your feet, bend and extend your legs, or pump your calves. Compression socks can help, too.

4. **THE SYMPTOMS.** If you are experiencing deep-vein thrombosis (DVT)—a dangerous clot in your extremities—you may feel like you have a persistent charley horse in your calf, groin, upper arm, or neck. You may experience redness or swelling, and the area might be warm to the touch. With a pulmonary embolism (PE)—a potentially fatal clot in your lung—you may be short of breath or feel faint, with a rapid heart rate or a crampy feeling in your side or chest. It may hurt to breathe.

5. **WHAT TO DO IF YOU HAVE SYMPTOMS.** Go to the emergency room. When in doubt, get checked out.

TWENTY-NINE

PREGNANCY

THE 7 RULES OF RUNNING WHILE TRYING TO CONCEIVE[1]

Oh, baby: You'd like to reproduce. The most important thing to know is that being physically fit and active, in most cases, is a boon to fertility. (Score!) Consider this stuff, too.

1. **THERE'S NO SET MILEAGE GUIDELINE.** Some pro runners get pregnant even while running upwards of 100 miles per week, while some women struggle at much lower thresholds. You won't know until you try which camp you're in.

2. **YOU NEED YOUR PERIOD.** Abnormal or absent cycles, a common issue in runners, are a problem. Regular cycles last between 22 and 33 days for women under 35. Your cycle can take a few months to stabilize if you're coming off hormonal birth control. If it's still wonky, consult your doctor: You may simply need to gain a few pounds (even if you're not technically underweight) to right the ship.

3. **TIME IT RIGHT.** You usually release one egg each month, and there's a limited window around ovulation when you can conceive. While more specific strategies exist, like tracking your

basal body temperature and observing your cervical fluid, having sex about every other day for a couple weeks starting a week to 10 days after your last period began should do it. You may need to stay flexible about when and how much you run to fit this in.

4. **BE PATIENT.** It can be hard to plan a training and racing schedule around a baby, because you never know when one might show up. If you're under 35, it's normal to take up to a year to conceive. Women between 35 and 40 should try for 6 months before consulting a doc; women over 40 should only wait 3.

5. **TAKE A TEST.** If you're still concerned, you can buy an ovulation predictor kit (available at drugstores or online) to see if you can detect a spike in luteinizing hormone, which is released just before you ovulate. If you can, you're likely in the clear to continue your current workout routine.

6. **CONSIDER YOUR PARTNER.** Working out in hot conditions can harm his swimmers, as can cycling. If you know you're ovulating and you've not seen success, it's easy to test his sperm.

7. **IF YOU DO HAVE TO CUT BACK . . .** We get it: It's stressful for runners to run less than they want to. Cope by introducing yoga, meditation, or gentle cross-training into your schedule—getting out for a long hike might fill the void left by giving up long runs.

THE 3 RULES OF RUNNING DURING PREGNANCY[2]

There will always be folks who scowl in your direction as you run by with your baby bump. We say, screw 'em. These rules are pretty obvious, but they're mostly here so you can show your judgmental family member or friend that the miles you log during pregnancy are none of their damn business.

1. **LISTEN TO YOUR DOCTOR.** In normal pregnancies, doctors encourage moderate exercise. Ask your doctor to evaluate your

routine. He or she is the only person other than you who needs to approve of your running.

2. **LISTEN TO YOUR BODY.** Every woman is different. Some can continue running, albeit more slowly than usual, up until their due date, while others find it too uncomfortable as ligaments loosen to prepare for childbirth. If you're no longer enjoying your running due to aches and pains, try downshifting to run-walking or walking, or give a low-impact form of cross-training a shot.

3. **STAY COOL.** On hot or humid days, especially during the first trimester, hit the treadmill—it's unlikely exercise alone will increase your body temperature to unsafe levels, but err on the side of caution. You'll also want to avoid hot tubs, saunas, and hot yoga.

THE 7 RULES OF RETURNING TO RUNNING AFTER PREGNANCY

First of all, congratulations! You have grown and birthed a tiny human, so we already know your body is damn impressive. Still, it needs some time to revert back to normal—maybe even more time than it takes your mind and schedule to adjust to having a newborn at home. If you're feeling ready to run again, read this first.

1. **WAIT FOR YOUR DOCTOR'S CLEARANCE . . .** [3] You'll likely have to wait about 6 to 8 weeks after giving birth to resume running. Until you get the go-ahead from your doctor to run, stick to walking or light strength training.

2. **. . . BUT THEN, TRUST IT.**[4] Your doctor will err on the side of caution. If he or she says you're good to go, you are. Don't be too afraid to ease back into your routine.

3. **GET NEW BRAS.**[5] You're likely to need more support than you did prepregnancy, especially if you're breastfeeding. See "5 Steps to Finding Your Perfect Sports Bra" (page 102) for fit guidelines.

4. **BE REALISTIC.**[6] A good rule of thumb is to expect to spend 9 months postpartum getting back to where you were before giving birth.

5. **EASE IN.**[7] Shoot for 30 minutes of exercise—either running or otherwise—daily. On run days, start by running 1 minute and walking 4 minutes, listening to your body as you gradually move toward running more and walking less.

6. **EAT AND DRINK RIGHT.**[8] If you're breastfeeding, continue taking your prenatal vitamins. Ask your doctor whether you should be taking any other supplements to support breastfeeding while running. Rehydrate after pumping and after running to ensure you continue to produce enough milk.

7. **STRENGTHEN KEY AREAS.** Hip and core strengthening exercises such as bridges, planks, and donkey kicks can keep you healthy as you ease back in,[9] but simply aim to fit in what you can—5 minutes at a time should suffice. The exception is if you're dealing with ab separation or incontinence. Then see an expert for a rehab routine.[10]

SECTION 6

157 RACING TIPS

THE 4 GOLDEN RULES OF RACING

---

1. **NOTHING NEW ON RACE DAY.**[1] This is the big one. If you haven't worn it, eaten it, drunk it, or otherwise used it in training, stay away from it on race day. You never know whether the new singlet will chafe or the new gel flavor will taste like sadness until you're trying it on a run—so try it on a run you *didn't* pay to do.

2. **PERFECT YOUR RACE-MORNING SCHEDULE.** The better prepared you are, the less likely you'll be to compound your race-day stress with, say, a nervous breakdown over not being able to find a parking space. Know exactly where you need to be, when you need to be there, how you're getting there, everything you need to do before the gun goes off, and about how long it all will take.[2]

3. **THE SHORTER AND FASTER THE RACE, THE LONGER AND MORE THOROUGH THE WARMUP SHOULD BE.**[3] To run your best 5K, you'll need to warm up for almost as long (or longer than) the race will take you, with jogging, strides, and dynamic stretches. For a marathon, though, you can simply ease in for the first few miles.

4. **DON'T GO OUT TOO FAST.** It's hard to avoid when you're well rested and high on adrenaline, but this common mistake can derail a race. If you don't feel like you're maybe going a little bit too slow in the first mile, you're probably going too fast.

THE 10 GOLDEN RULES OF RACE-DAY ETIQUETTE[4]

Unless you're a big-city runner, you likely don't train in the types of crowds you'll be among on race day. Here's how to avoid being "that guy" fellow racers silently seethe about en route to the finish line.

1. **SEED YOURSELF CORRECTLY.** Sure, we're all runners, regardless of how fast we can move—but that doesn't mean we all belong directly on the starting line. If you're pretty confident everyone around you is going to beat you to the finish, you need to line up farther back. (And if a race asks for a past PR or a goal time for seeding purposes when you register, be honest and realistic.)
2. **KEEP YOUR PACE.** Don't run right off the shoulder of another runner—unless he or she is an official pace group leader, and even then, give 'em a little space. And just like on the highway, if you speed up every time someone tries to pass you, that's annoying AF.
3. **PIPE DOWN.** The similarly paced people around you may not be able to get away, so be considerate. Use headphones if you're listening to music, have conversations in a low voice, and if your keys jingle loudly with every step, try to stow them more securely.
4. **CHECK YOUR MIRRORS.** If you need to move laterally, look over your shoulder before you do it. At aid stations, you're less likely to cut people off if you wait until the middle or end of the station to take water or fuel.
5. **NO SUDDEN STOPS.** If you're taking walk breaks, pull over to one side of the road, raise your hand, and announce, "Walk break!" or "I'm stopping!" before slowing.
6. **QUIT FIDDLING WITH YOUR PHONE.** Weaving all over the road as you change playlists or text your spectators an update

is not okay. And if you drop your phone and shatter your screen as you're posing for your umpteenth midrace selfie, don't expect sympathy from the runners who've been trying to dodge your outstretched arm for the past 10 miles.

7. **WATCH YOUR FLUIDS.** Look around before spitting or snot-rocketing. When in doubt, it's better to hit yourself than to hit a stranger. And avoid dropping half-full cups of water or sports drink on other runners' feet.

8. **TRY NOT TO REEK.** None of us smells fresh as a daisy while we're racing, but please, roll on some deodorant prerun and don't douse yourself in perfume, cologne, or "body spray." And if you're gassy . . . maybe try to stay near the sidelines.

9. **PICK UP ON SOCIAL CUES.** Headphones are one clue that a fellow racer isn't interested in chatting. One-word answers are another. Take a hint!

10. **KEEP MOVING THROUGH THE CHUTE.** Sure, after you finish, it's dramatic to stop and pant and rest your hands on your knees— but you're blocking the progress of less theatrical runners. Get out of the way first.

> **BONUS TIP** If you *must* propose at a finish line, move through the chute before you drop to one knee. Race directors don't appreciate your special moment clogging up the flow.[5]

THIRTY

PRERACE KNOW-HOW

6 THINGS TO DO IN THE WEEK LEADING UP TO RACE DAY[1]

Even experienced runners may have a brain fart in the exciting and anxiety-ridden days before a big event. Keep this checklist on hand to ensure you don't forget anything important.

1. **MAKE ANOTHER LIST.** Your packing list, that is—what you'll bring for the weekend, if you're traveling, and what you'll bring to the starting line if you're running closer to home. There's no such thing as overpacking for a race, so be prepared for every possible weather condition or health hiccup.

2. **HIT GOAL PACE.** If you do any running faster than easy during these 7 days—and you should, unless your goal is only to finish—do it at race pace. You needn't do a lot, but the idea is to set your autopilot so you're under control when the gun goes off.

3. **STUDY THE COURSE.** Examining the map and elevation profile is good, but driving the route is better. You don't want late-race hills or other challenges to take you by surprise.

4. **DO A SHAKEOUT.** A 20- to 30-minute easy run the day before

the event can burn off some nerves and help you sleep better that night.

5. **TOTE YOUR FUEL.** If you're traveling, stock a backpack with all the foods and drinks that have proven to be safe during training. Have a water bottle in hand at all times to ensure you're staying hydrated.

6. **LAY OUT FLAT YOU.** Assemble your outfit, fuel, supplies, and number/chip the evening before the race. It's better to realize you're missing something *now*. The Instagram photo of Flat (Insert Your Name Here) is optional—but if you do it, consider placing something on your bib to obscure the full number, as sophisticated counterfeiters have been known to snag and duplicate bibs from social media posts.

3 REASONS TO NEVER, EVER WEAR SOMEONE ELSE'S BIB IN A RACE . . . [2]

Some races have bib-transfer programs, in which one runner can *legally* give or sell his or her number to another runner. We are *not* referring to those circumstances here. We're talking about the all-too-common practice of running with a friend's bib or buying one from Craigslist. If you're not sure what the big deal is, let us enlighten you.

1. **IT'S DANGEROUS FOR YOU.** Even if you're a healthy, physically fit person, you could still need medical attention on the course. If you can't respond, and you're running with a bib registered to someone else's name, officials will try to reach the original registrant's emergency contact—which won't help you and may unnecessarily alarm someone else.

2. **YOU COULD MESS UP THE RESULTS.** If your bib is registered to someone outside your age group, or of the opposite sex, you could potentially "win" a prize you did not earn—bumping out a runner who actually deserved it.

3. **YOU COULD GET BANNED.** Some races and organizers have strict rules about bib-swapping. If you're caught, you might be banned from that event (or all events put on by that organization) for life.

. . . AND 3 REASONS TO NEVER, EVER GIVE OR SELL YOUR BIB TO SOMEONE ELSE[3]

It's just as wrong to be on this end of this transaction. Here's why.

1. **IT MAKES YOU A CHEATER . . .** Give your bib to a faster runner, and the world will think you're speedier than you are—results live on the Internet forever, you know. Even worse is using a faster runner's time under your name to register for a race that has time requirements (such as the Boston Marathon), or that lets faster runners register early or get guaranteed entry.

2. **. . . OR IT MESSES UP YOUR REP.** Give your bib to a slower runner, and that result will *also* live on the Internet forever.

3. **YOU COULD GET BANNED.** It's actually easier for you to get caught—you put in your personal info to get the bib. If organizers with rules against swapping notice that, say, a man wearing your bib was the "first female" to cross the line, they know the name and contact information for at least one of the parties at fault. (You!)

5 REASONS TO ATTEND AN EXPO EVEN IF YOU'RE NOT RACING[4]

If you didn't win the lottery for the big race nearest you, take the money you saved on registration and head to the expo for:

1. **DISCOUNTED STUFF.** You can probably find shoes you already know you like for even less than you'd pay online. Same goes for apparel, accessories, and fuel. Shop around before shelling out, as several booths may have the same item at different price points.
2. **DISCOUNTED RACES.** Some events offer discounts to expo attendees, while others raffle off free entries or other swag—just be prepared to provide your contact info.
3. **FREE STUFF.** Scoop up samples and coupons—they're not just for registered runners. An added bonus: You can try *all* the snacks without fretting that your angry stomach will ruin a race.
4. **NEW FRIENDS.** Local running clubs will likely have a presence at the expo. If you're new to an area or looking to expand beyond your go-to group runs, an expo's a great place to start.
5. **EXPERT ADVICE.** Some expos offer general seminars on training, nutrition, and injury prevention in addition to race-specific ones. You also may find booths featuring local massage therapists, physical therapists, and sports-medicine docs you can interview before making an appointment.

4 QUESTIONS TO ASK YOUR PACER AT THE EXPO[5]

Even though you can't *really* know how good your pacer is until you're actually running together, it won't hurt to stop by the pace team booth to see if you can meet him or her prerace. Here's what to find out.

1. **CAN YOU TELL ME A LITTLE BIT ABOUT YOURSELF?** Try to learn whether this person has paced this (or other) races before and what their fastest times are. Someone who's led the sub-4:00 group at Your Hometown Marathon for the last 10 years must be doing something right, but a first-time pacer for the sub-4:00 group who's never run *this* race but has run a few marathons with a best time of 3:55 is less encouraging.

2. **WHAT'S YOUR STRATEGY?** Some pacers are like metronomes—they run the same pace for every single mile. Others try to work with the course a bit more, by slowing a bit on long uphill stretches and making it up on the downhills. Neither way is right or wrong, but know what you're getting into before you tag along.

3. **HOW DO YOU INTERACT WITH THE PEOPLE IN YOUR GROUPS?** If you're dealing with one of the rare "I like to bark encouragement at the people around me in a loud voice" leaders, it's good to know that in advance. Once you've committed to a crew, you can't escape without speeding up or slowing down.

> **BONUS TIP** To "shakeout run" or not to "shakeout run"? (That's the term usually used to refer to a short, easy run the day before a big race.) If you're feeling fatigued, don't do it. If you're antsy with nerves, head out for 20 to 30 minutes, supereasy, to loosen up muscles and prime your body and mind to race the following day.[6]

4. **CAN I HAVE ONE OF THESE PACE BRACELETS?** Sometimes pace group tables offer free bracelets with the time you need to hit at each mile to make your goal. Snag one—it's good backup in case you end up flying solo.

---

6 ITEMS TO PACK IN YOUR GEAR-CHECK BAG . . . [7]

---

1. **TOILET PAPER.** Always cram some extra TP in your bag and in the pockets of your race attire—you never know when you'll hit a porta-potty that's out.
2. **PETROLEUM JELLY/ANTICHAFING BALM.** Lube up as you wait to start and apply to any hot spots postrace for some relief. Petroleum jelly works to soothe chapped lips and skin, too.
3. **SNACKS AND BEVVIES.** You'll want whatever fuel you need for midrace—just don't forget to put it in your pockets or belt before you start running. And remember to pack anything special you want afterward. (Tiny bottle of celebratory champagne, anyone?)
4. **DRY CLOTHES.** Change ASAP after you claim your gear bag. Sweaty clothes aren't fun to wear once you're no longer running. Pack more layers than you think you'll need to avoid feeling chilled.
5. **DRY, COMFY SHOES.** It feels awfully good to take off shoes you've been sweating into for 13.1 (or 26.2) miles. This is also important if you're doing a shorter race in the rain—waterlogged kicks can cause blisters.
6. **SMELL-GOODS.** We're talking body wipes, deodorant, or anything else that might make you less offensive to the people you encounter until you're able to take a shower. (And who wants to take a shower when postrace brunch awaits?)

... AND 4 ITEMS TO KEEP ON YOUR PERSON (OR LEAVE WITH YOUR CHEER SQUAD)[8]

IDENTIFICATION, CELL PHONE, MEDICATIONS, KEYS. It's rare, but gear-check bags can get misplaced or lost. Murphy's Law says this will only happen if you put something really valuable in there, so stick to easily replaceable, inexpensive items, just in case.

BONUS TIP Research shows that you're physically capable of performing just as well after a night of bad sleep as you do well rested, so don't stress if you're lying awake on race-day eve (or if you have to rise at an ungodly hour to make it to the start).[9]

THIRTY-ONE

RACE-MORNING TRICKS

8 WAYS TO SEEM LIKE YOU KNOW WHAT YOU'RE DOING AT YOUR FIRST RACE[1]

If the idea of racing intimidates you, registering is a big first step. Once you've done that, it's a waste of money to not show up! Here's how to ensure no one at the expo or event even notices that you're a noob.

1. **KNOW WHERE YOU'RE GOING.** The event website will tell you where you need to be and when to pick up your race number (also known as a "bib") and to run the race. These details are second in importance only to how far the race is. Bonus points if you also check out the course map and do a little training on the race route, so you know what you're up against.

2. **PICK UP YOUR BIB (AND CHIP).** This may take place race morning *or* the day before the race. You may need to bring identification. If you received an e-mail about your bib number, you may need to bring that too. If you're running a large enough race, your bib might have an electronic timing chip attached to it, or you might receive one to place on your shoes.

3. **REMEMBER TO WEAR YOUR BIB (AND CHIP).** A rookie mistake that even experienced runners make is to forget one or both of these things on race morning. A bib is how organizers know you've paid to run an event. If a chip is provided, that's how they time you. If you remember nothing else, remember these things! (And your running shoes, of course.)

4. **ARRIVE EARLY.** Plan to be all settled in the start area at least an hour before gun time. Even if you're not doing much of a warmup—and you may not, if your goal is just to finish—you'll likely want to whizz.

5. **BRING SOMETHING TO SIT ON WHILE YOU WAIT.** A trash bag works to prevent soggy butt.

6. **LINE UP EARLY, AND TOWARD THE BACK.** Larger races may have corrals, which are sectioned-off portions of the start area meant to group runners of similar paces. If you've been assigned one, line up there when the announcers tell you to. If the start area's a free-for-all, err on the side of caution and choose a spot farther back. It's good manners (and smart for safety) to stay out of the way of faster runners.

7. **RUN CONSERVATIVELY.** Nothing screams first-time racer like someone who sprints for 100 meters and then slows to a walk. Meter your effort and avoid running too much faster than you do in training for the first portions of the race.

8. **FINISH STRONG AND SMART.** If you're feeling good toward the end, you can push a bit harder. Just remember that you'll want to cross the line upright and smiling so you can continue moving through the finishing chute.

4 NO-GEAR-CHECK-REQUIRED WAYS TO STAY WARM AND/OR DRY ON THE STARTING LINE

1. **AN OLD SPACE BLANKET.** Save it from one race to use at the next.

2. **A TRASH BAG.** Arm holes, optional. Head hole, required.

3. **THROWAWAY CLOTHES.** An old ratty sweatshirt you own or an old ratty sweatshirt from Goodwill: Either one works.

4. **DIY ARM WARMERS.** Give worn-out tall socks a new life by cutting a hole in the toe end to make them arm warmers, or wear them as is for long quasi-mittens.

BONUS TIP Wrap that space blanket around your waist (or entire body) and find a clear patch of grass to kneel in. Voilà: the most portable porta-potty in existence. (Not recommended for number twos.)[2]

6 WAYS TO ENSURE YOU STOP POOPING BEFORE YOU START RACING

No one *wants* to use the porta-potties along race courses, but the clock stops for no one—and for no number two, either. The potties are there for the poor, unfortunate souls who *didn't* learn how to prevent a *poop*-tastrophe—or how to stop one in its tracks.

1. **WATCH WHAT YOU EAT AND DRINK IN THE DAYS PRIOR.** Even the common strategy of carbo-loading can spell intestinal disaster if you eat the wrong things. (And for some people, pasta—surprise!—may be a "wrong thing.") You might be able to determine your gut triggers in training, but if you've

missed that window, avoid the common culprits of dairy products, artificial sweeteners, soy, eggs, caffeine, and gluten[3] just to be safe. Also limit your intake of foods high in fat and fiber.[4]

2. **WATCH HOW MUCH YOU EAT, TOO.** It's simple. More food in equals more poop out. Carbo-loading doesn't mean eating *more* calories—it means getting a greater proportion of those calories from carbohydrates.[5] You should leave meals the day before the race feeling sated but not stuffed.

3. **SKIP THE COFFEE.** Even if it's usually okay in training, it can enrage a nervous stomach. If you must have morning caffeine to function, take a caffeinated gel or two prerace.[6] This format is easier on your innards.

4. **CALM YOURSELF.** Deep breathing or listening to relaxing music prerace can help limit the laxative effects of adrenaline.[7] Looking at a course map and knowing exactly where the potties are might soothe your mind enough that you won't have to use them.

5. **FUEL SLOWLY.** Taking in small sips of gel or sports drink (followed by small sips of water) on the course can ensure you don't overexcite your digestive system or swallow air that can cause gas and bloating.[8]

6. **MEDICATE.** Desperate times call for antidiarrheal medications—if you've tried them in training. Start with a half or quarter dose and avoid taking so much that you're constipated postrun.[9]

---

4 BIB-SECURING OPTIONS
FOR THE SAFETY-PINLESS

---

1. **USE YOUR EARRINGS.**
2. **TUCK IT UNDER YOUR SPORTS BRA BAND . . .**
3. **. . . OR ROLL IT UNDER YOUR WAISTBAND.**

4. **BEG FOR STRANGERS' MERCY.** Not everyone needs four! Try to bum just one off two different people.

4 WARMUPS THAT'LL READY YOU TO RACE[10]

It doesn't matter how well you've trained: If you screw up your warmup, you won't run your fastest. Luckily, you're reading this! Here's how to ace your prerace routine no matter which distance you're targeting. All of these should be completed as close to go time as possible—once you know what to do, getting the timing right is the hardest part.

1. **ONE MILE.** Plan to spend a *lot* more time warming up than the race will actually take you, because you're going to run so! fast! Start by jogging for about 25 minutes, then do five to eight 80- to 90-meter strides, accelerating to close to your mile-race pace at the peak of each. Follow that with whichever dynamic stretches you do before speedwork. Walking lunges, leg swings, and skips are all good options.

2. **5K/10K.** You can jog a little bit less here—15 minutes or so—and then launch into cutback strides: Do six or eight total, with the first couple longer and slower (about 200 meters, ramping up gradually to race pace) and the last couple shorter and faster (about 50 meters, ramping up quickly to race pace). If you do dynamic stretches before speedwork, do them now, too.

3. **HALF MARATHON.** Ten to 15 minutes of jogging, plus four 200-meter strides ramping up just to half-marathon pace, will suffice. Because the race is fairly long, you don't want to shoot off the line, so plan to spend the first mile or so easing into your pace. You may end up hitting goal pace anyway, but the intention to hold back will at least keep you from starting too fast.

4. **FULL MARATHON.** If you're reading this, you're probably not a professional runner. (If you are, shouldn't you be napping or something? It's part of your job—lucky you!) Only the pros need to warm up before such a long race. Instead, run the first few miles 2 to 5 percent slower than your goal pace as an in-race "warmup," then settle into your planned pace.

THIRTY-TWO

MIDRACE TACTICS

---

4 COMMON RACING MISTAKES (AND HOW TO AVOID MAKING THEM)[1]

Too many runners have race-day stage fright. You completely nail rehearsals, but when it actually matters, you forget all your lines and barely dodge the rotten produce your inner critic hurls at you. Well, never again.

1. **GOING OUT TOO FAST.** You haven't learned to meter your pace in the face of race-day excitement and/or anxiety. During your next training cycle, schedule regular tune-up races of various distances in which your *only* objective is to go out at the pace you plan to run in your goal race.

2. **GETTING A SIDE STITCH.** Going out too fast is one way to get a stitch. Improper prerace fueling is another. Races that last longer than an hour require a full prerace meal of at least 300 calories, which means you need enough time to digest—3 to 4 hours. You can eat a low-fat, low-fiber snack of 200 to 250 calories 2 hours before shorter races. Test out prerace meals and their timing before at least two training runs at race pace to make sure the food sits well. See "3 Ways to Erase a

Side Stitch without Stopping" (page 20) to learn what to do when it's too late for prevention.

3. **MIDRUN FUELING MISHAPS.** You only need to take in calories if you're racing for longer than an hour or so. The goal is to consume 30 to 60 grams of carbs per hour, but you need to train your stomach to process that fuel *while you're holding race pace*—a gel that works on long, easy runs may cause nausea when you speed up. Try lots of products to find your best match. Once you do, practice: Spreading out your intake by taking 5 to 10 minutes to finish a gel may improve absorption and reduce queasiness.

4. **EXTREME NERVES.** Frequent tune-up racing can help quell nerves, as can being punctual and prepared for the start. Then take a few deep breaths and remember that butterflies are a sign that your body is primed to run its hardest and best. If you're so nervous that you're vomiting or experiencing diarrhea, look to your diet. Overeating or consuming too many hard-to-digest foods in the days leading up to the race is likely to blame.

4 WAYS TO AVOID A TOO-FAST START[2]

So many runners—even experienced ones!—blast off at the starting gun and eventually crap out. The longer your race, the more problematic this is, as you're squandering energy stores you'll need later on and taxing muscles that still have a long way to carry you. A controlled start is best developed by frequent practice in a race environment, but these tactics can help, too.

1. **SEED YOURSELF WISELY.** If your race doesn't have corrals, look for signage that corresponds with your planned pace per mile and line up near there. If your race lacks those, you're going to have to guess. When in doubt, err on the side of lining up farther back—especially in a half or full marathon.

2. **FOLLOW A PACER.** Many half and full marathons provide

pacers. Find one that's running slightly slower than your goal pace and stick with them for the first few miles.

BONUS TIP In most races, your goal should be to achieve a "negative split," which means running the second half faster than the first. To get there, borrow this mantra coined by *Runner's World* contributing editor Scott Douglas: "In the first half of the race, don't be an idiot. In the second half, don't be a wimp."[3]

3. **CHECK YOUR WATCH.** GPS watches allow you to track your pace in real time, though this function can be a little erratic. For better accuracy, use the "lap pace" function and use the "split" button as you pass each mile marker.[4]

4. **USE A MANTRA.** Repeating calming mantras like "relax" or "save it" as you ease into your race can help neutralize the effects of starting-line adrenaline.

3 PROS (AND 3 CONS) OF JOINING A PACE GROUP[5]

At the start of many half and full marathons, you'll see a few runners holding really long sticks with signs on top announcing their goal times. No, they're not just looking for extra accountability along the course. They're pace group leaders, which means their purpose is to help other runners reach their goals. Each leader should be capable of racing much faster than the group they're heading up; their group's pace should be relatively easy for them to hit consistently, mile after mile. You don't have to sign up to join a pace group—you just latch on. Here's how to decide whether that's a good idea.

1. **PRO: YOU CAN TURN OFF YOUR BRAIN.** The best pacers hit every mile marker within a few seconds of goal pace, like magical robots engineered to help everyday people break 2 hours in a half or qualify for Boston. If your pacer is a good one, you can stop looking at your watch and simply follow. All

the mental energy you can save early in the race will come in handy when the going gets tough.

2. **PRO: YOU GET A "TEAM."** Pace group members and leaders often develop a rapport as the race goes on. Swapping stories helps the early miles pass more quickly, and leaders may offer support and encouragement if you're struggling later.

3. **PRO: YOU CAN DRAFT.** This only makes a difference when there's a significant headwind or crosswind—most of us aren't fast enough to face much wind resistance on calm days.[6]

1. **CON: THEY'RE NOT AVAILABLE FOR ALL GOAL TIMES.** The goal times for pace groups may be spaced out every 5, 10, or 15 minutes. If yours isn't available, you're SOL.

2. **CON: YOU NEVER KNOW WHO YOU'RE GONNA GET.** If your pacer isn't a magical robot, watch out: The worst pacers take their groups out way too fast and may not manage to finish under the goal time themselves. Unfortunately, you don't really know until you get out there, so keep an eye on your watch for the first few miles. If a pace feels too hard, let the group go—you can always reel them in later.

3. **CON: YOU MAY DEAL WITH CROWDS.** The groups for popular goal times (a sub-2:00 half, for example, or a sub-4:00 marathon) in large races can be *enormous*. This can mean "flat tires" from runners following too closely behind you, competition at aid stations, and difficulty escaping people who are blasting bad music or wearing stinky cologne. The group will most likely thin out as the race goes on, so hang in there if the pacer is helping you.

3 STRATEGIES FOR RACING NAKED (THAT IS, WITHOUT A GPS DEVICE)[7]

If you've ever experienced postrace neck soreness from repetitive watch-glancing, it's time for an intervention. It is possible—and in some cases, even more likely—that you'll race your best by leaving your device at home. (Gasp!) If you've been unhappy with your data-driven performances, it's worth a shot. Here's how to try it.

> **BONUS TIP** As you crest a hill, take 10 short, quick steps to avoid the slowdown many runners experience.[8]

1. **NOTICE YOUR BREATHING.** Your body has a built-in effort-monitoring system: your inhales and exhales. If you're able to maintain a conversation, you're running easy. If you can manage a few words at a time, that's approximately tempo pace. If a few words are difficult, you're getting into speed-work territory. Learning to distinguish between easy, moderate, and hard efforts is step one. Then try shifting between them in workouts. Try 10 easy minutes to warm up, 10 minutes at a moderate effort, and then alternating 1 minute at an easy effort and 1 minute at a hard effort.

2. **TRY IT IN TUNE-UPS.** Schedule a couple shorter races (5K to 10K) before your big event where you can practice gauging your effort in a competitive environment. Warm up at an easy effort, start out at a moderate effort, and gradually ramp up to a hard effort.

3. **DEPLOY IT ON RACE DAY.** If you can still wear your GPS watch and check it only every few miles, fine—but most people can't resist frequent peeks. You can wear a regular watch or rely on race clocks or pace groups to have a sense of time without being obsessive, but staying in touch with your breathing and perceived effort will ensure you run your best race on that day.

3 TACTICS TO EMPLOY WHEN THE GOING GETS TOUGH[9]

If you're truly racing, you will start struggling to keep the pace at some point. Congrats! You're doing it right! When that moment arrives, be prepared to do one of these.

1. **HAVE A "CALM CONVERSATION."**[10] This tip comes from coach Steve Magness, who works with pros, collegiate runners, and everyday folks. If you find yourself having a freak-out moment thinking "I can't keep this up!" or "This is so hard!" change your inner monologue to something like, "This hurts, but that's okay. It just means I'm running my fastest." Practice this strategy on hard training runs to *really* master it.

2. **RECALL WHAT YOU'VE SACRIFICED.** Now's the time to remember all those early-morning workouts, all the happy hours you skipped, all the time you invested in training instead of in something else. Recalling what you gave up to race your best might boost your motivation to make the most of your hard work.

3. **START THANKING PEOPLE.** Research shows that feeling and showing gratitude has a positive effect on your perception of effort and pain. Luckily, race day presents ample opportunities to say thank you. The volunteers at water stops, the police officers stopping traffic, the spectators with clever signs—smile and tell them you're grateful, and you'll feel better than you would if you gritted your teeth and sulked.

> **BONUS TIP** The best way to down water or sports drink quickly (without spilling it all over yourself or choking) is to pinch the cup to form a spout.[11]

3 WAYS TO ENDURE CHAFING AND BLISTERS ONCE IT'S TOO LATE

If you didn't adequately lube up prerace—especially on wet or sweaty days—you may be suffering from more than just fatigue midway through. Here's how to lessen the pain.

1. **GRAB SOME PETROLEUM JELLY.** Many longer races have volunteers holding out tongue depressors smeared with blobs of Vaseline. Delirious racers have been known to think this is

some kind of energy gel and to eat it.[12] Don't do that! Instead, smear it on affected areas. If this means stopping to remove your shoes and socks, do it. You'll make up the time if you can run without discomfort.

2. **RECYCLE.** If you're limping from a blister, slip an empty gel packet between the irritated skin and your sock to reduce friction.[13]

3. **HIT A MEDICAL TENT.** If blisters or chafing are affecting your gait, and no other solution is working, stop for professional help. Logging serious miles with an altered stride can lead to injuries that may last long after your raw skin has healed.

THE 7 RULES OF NOT RACING LIKE AN IDIOT IN THE HEAT[14]

A hotter-than-expected race day is like a disappointing blind date: Once you're there, you just have to hang in and make it to the end. However, an unpleasant conversation filled with awkward silences is far less dangerous than the heat-related illnesses that can strike during or after a sweltering race. Here's how to make the best of this bad situation.

1. **LOWER YOUR EXPECTATIONS.** If you think the heat won't slow you down, you're just wrong. For most people, performance starts to suffer above about 50° to 60°F. You can expect to slow by about 20 to 30 seconds per mile for every 5 degrees the temperature rises above 60.

2. **RUN BY FEEL.** Instead of locking in on a new goal pace based on the temperature and the aforementioned rule of thumb, ditch the watch and tune in to your body. Everyone reacts to heat differently, so your pace may end up being faster (or slower) than your heat-adjusted estimation. Maintain the effort level you remember from workouts at race pace in cooler weather.

3. **HYDRATE WELL . . .** This means taking in enough fluids in the days leading up to the race *and* on race morning. You'll want some water and some sports drink with electrolytes, which help you absorb the fluids you're ingesting. Don't overdo it, though—your pee should be light yellow, not clear.

4. **. . . AND AVOID DIURETICS.** Alcohol, antihistamines, and caffeine all encourage more frequent urination, which can lead to dehydration. If skipping prerun coffee sounds unthinkable, consider drinking just enough to hold off a withdrawal headache.

5. **COVER UP.** To avoid a nasty sunburn, wear a sweatproof sunscreen with an SPF of 30-plus, a hat or visor, sunglasses, and lightweight wicking clothing. Light colors and mesh keep you cooler but may not protect the skin beneath from UV rays. If you can see light through an article of clothing, apply sunscreen underneath it.

6. **LUBE UP.** Sweat equals soaked clothes equals a high likelihood of chafing and blisters. Don't skimp on the antichafing balm and/or petroleum jelly.

7. **STAY WET.** At each aid station, dump a cup of water over your head. Keep drinking, too, and slow down or walk through stations if that'll help you get the fluids you need.

> **BONUS TIP** The cure for a bonk is usually to take in some calories, but if your stomach is raging, try swishing some sports drink in your mouth and spitting it out. Research shows that this gives your body and brain a temporary boost.[15]

THIRTY-THREE

POSTRACE CONSIDERATIONS

---

3 WAYS TO COPE WITH THE POSTRACE BLUES[1]

When you've trained for weeks (or months) for a single day, and that day has come and gone, ita's normal to feel some angst—even if you crushed your goal. Scaling back your miles to recover means fewer exercise-induced feel-good chemicals coursing through your brain. If you ran well, you may be wondering if you'll ever race that well again. If you ran poorly, you may be beating yourself up. Stop doing that and start doing these things instead.

1. **ENJOY THE REST.** What are some things you put on pause as you trained? Are there friends you haven't seen in a while? A book you've been meaning to devour? A TV series you've been hankering to binge? Indulge in the activities you put aside during training and make your downtime as pleasant as possible. This typically means turning off the alarm and logging some extra shut-eye, too.

2. **ANALYZE YOUR PERFORMANCE.** Figure out what did and didn't work in terms of training, nutrition, and racing so you can repeat the good things (and avoid the same mistakes) in the future. Don't dwell, though, and don't let other people

bring you down. If someone asks you about the race and you don't want to talk about it, a simple "I'm happy with my effort" will suffice, even if that's not entirely true.

3. **CHOOSE YOUR NEXT GOAL.** Wait until the idea of training for another event truly excites you before signing up for one. Not happening? Set your sights elsewhere. Perhaps you'd like to learn better swim technique so you can eventually tackle a tri, or to build up your upper body so you're less easily identified as an endurance athlete. As long as you're doing some running as a supplement to your other fitness goals, you'll be able to come back to race training when you're ready.

---

3 SIGNS YOU'RE RACING TOO MUCH . . . [2]

Contrary to what members of groups like the Marathon or Half Marathon Maniacs might tell you, it *is* possible to run too many races. Here's how to know if you're overdoing it.

1. **YOUR PERFORMANCE IS SUFFERING.** If your times at a given distance on similar courses are getting progressively slower over the course of a year, that's a red flag. Make each event count by preceding it with a proper training cycle that includes no more than one tune-up race.

2. **YOU'RE DREADING RACE DAY.** Racing is supposed to be a fun challenge. You may enjoy it more if you choose just one all-out goal race per season and use others as tune-ups, where you can practice fueling, pacing, and dealing with crowds. If you still hate racing—just don't do it! You're no less of a runner if you log miles without competing.

3. **YOUR BANK BALANCES ARE DANGEROUSLY LOW.** Races can be expensive, especially ones with on-course music, fancy medals, and elaborate postrace parties. Spending more than 10 percent of your income on a hobby is excessive. Choose no-frills races or limit participation in pricey events to once or twice per year.

. . . AND 3 SIGNS YOU OUGHT
TO RACE MORE OFTEN[3]

There are plenty of good reasons to bib up somewhat regularly, and if you're not doing it, you likely won't ever race your best.

1. **EVERY RACE FEELS SO NERVE-RACKING.** You'll never learn to cope with prerace anxiety if you don't put yourself in that competitive environment. A couple build-up events before a true goal race can help you work out race-morning kinks and build confidence in your ability to deliver.

2. **YOU STOP RUNNING WITHOUT A GOAL.** If your training drops off dramatically when you're not registered for something, register for something—even if your goal is just to have fun and finish. Extended breaks cause you to lose fitness, and you'll need to get back into the habit of logging miles when you decide to train again.

3. **YOU'RE STILL NOT SURE HOW TO PIN ON A BIB.** If you ever want to race your best, you'll need to master the minutiae of race-day logistics: how to secure a number, time your portapotty visits, and arrive at the starting line warmed up. The only way to do it is to race somewhat regularly. Every few months or so will suffice.

3 THINGS FREQUENT RACERS
CAN GAIN FROM A BREAK[4]

1. **PERSPECTIVE.** It's hard to see the big picture when you're on the constant-racing hamster wheel. You may define yourself by only your most recent performance, causing you to set unrealistic goals if you just had a breakthrough race, or to doubt your ability to succeed if you recently raced like garbage.

2. **BALANCE.** Remember your family and nonrunning friends?

They probably remember you too, and might even miss spending time with you.

3. **ENERGY.** If you've been training for a distance race, you'll be amazed at all you can achieve on the weekends without a long run draining your battery. And not having a goal race on the horizon for a while can help build excitement and momentum for when you decide to register for something again.

5 WAYS TO DISPLAY YOUR RACE MEDALS, FROM LEAST TO MOST CREATIVE

You've worked hard for the medals, so hard for the medals—so you'd better show 'em off. If yours have ended up in a shoebox under your bed, take them out, dust them off, and try one of these ways to display them.

1. **BULLETIN BOARD.** You can pin them up along with your bibs for a simple shrine to your accomplishments. Bonus points if you do this in your office—you wouldn't want your coworkers to mistake you for a nonrunner, would you?

2. **SHADOW BOXES.** This is best when you have just a few special races you want to commemorate. You can add in your bib, photos from the race, and other memorabilia to create a memento suitable for hanging.

3. **CURTAIN RODS.** You probably don't want to use one that's also holding curtains. Instead, fix one up on a wall near your treadmill and thread it through the fabric loops attached to your medals. You can pin up bibs behind and around it to create a big display.

4. **CHRISTMAS TREE.**[5] Some runners use their medals as ornaments and their bibs as garland. Get an artificial tree and you can keep the self-celebratory spirit alive all year!

5. **MANNEQUIN TORSO.** You can buy these on the Internet—because what *can't* you buy on the Internet?—and loop the medals around the neck. If you really want to go all-out, you can clothe the mannequin in race bibs.[6]

THIRTY-FOUR

ADVICE FOR SPECIFIC RACES

5 TIPS FOR A PERFECT 5K[1]

It's the most popular distance *and* one of the toughest ones to master. Start here.

1. **SCOUT THE COURSE.** While a flat course might be most conducive to a PR, you can run fast on rollers if you know where they are. Jog the course a week before race day so you know when to expect a challenge—and when you can use gravity to your advantage.

2. **WARM UP SUPER WELL.** This means jogging for a *minimum* of 10 minutes, though 20 is better, and doing whatever dynamic stretches (leg swings, butt kicks, skips) you usually do before speedwork. After that, run a handful of strides (roughly 100-meter pickups) that peak right around your goal race pace. Time this so you're striding as close to the race's start time as you can manage. This is an easier feat in a smaller race.

3. **SEED YOURSELF WITH SMARTS.** Most 5Ks aren't large enough to have corrals or chip timing. Before you go to a race, check out the previous year's results to get a sense of how many people will finish ahead of you and try to line up with about that many people between you and the starting line.

4. **GO FOR IT.** It takes practice to find the balance between sprinting at the gun (don't do that!) and holding back too much in the first mile. If you've trained for speed and you're well rested, you'll likely feel like you're running just a little bit too slowly when you're actually hitting your goal pace.

5. **GUT IT OUT.** The second mile should feel like an eight out of 10 in terms of effort level, and the third, a 10 out of 10. (See why we said 5Ks are tough to master?) Try to remain calm and positive, using upbeat mantras like "I got this" or "feeling good" to trick your body and mind into holding a hard, fast pace.

7 RULES FOR RUNNING A REALLY HUGE RACE[2]

The largest races in the United States have tens of thousands of runners—and, more appealingly, even *more* spectators out cheering for friends and strangers. You could spend years trying to get into these popular events. Once you're in, here's what to do.

1. **REHEARSE THE PRERACE TIMING . . .** You might need to wake up really, really early to get to the start area on time, and you might be there for hours before your wave takes off. Do at least a couple dress-rehearsal long runs that involve waking up, eating, drinking, using the bathroom, and starting to run at the same time you'll do those things on race morning.

2. **. . . AND THE POSTRACE SLOG.** Many big-city races have a finishing chute that's a half mile long or longer. Then, to get back to your car or hotel, you may have to hoof it—if you're a midpacker, you'll have lots of competition for cabs or space on public transportation. After your rehearsal long runs, keep walking for a mile or so to practice.

3. **MAKE A TRANSPORTATION PLAN . . .** Some races, like the New York City Marathon, require you to choose in advance an approved way of reaching the start village. Others require a 26-mile bus ride to get there—that's the Boston

Marathon. Make sure you know how you're traveling, and if a long trip is involved, try one *Runner's World* writer's strategy: Before dress-rehearsal runs, practice napping upright in a chair.[3]

4. **. . . AND A FOOD PLAN.** For a longer race like a half or full marathon, eat a full meal 2 or 3 hours before your race, even if you're on a bus or in a start village at that time. You'll need to find a portable meal that works for you and doesn't require heating or refrigeration. Have a snack before your meal if you're famished when you arise.

5. **DRESS FOR SUCCESS.** Throwaway clothes are essential— there's a sometimes sizable lag between when you must check a bag and when you start running. Go to Goodwill and pick up some cozy stuff you won't mind tossing.

6. **ENLIST A FRIEND.** If you have throwaway clothes and a willing spectator, you might be able to hand him or her your postrace essentials and skip bag check entirely. This can help you pass through prerace security faster and skip the lines to retrieve your bag at the finish. Just make sure you have a very specific place to meet afterward: "Near the library" is bad; "under the only willow tree on the library's southern side" is perfect.

7. **LEARN TO REMAIN CALM.** You know what wastes a lot of energy? Weaving through the sea of humanity that'll clog up the first few miles of your big race. The longer you're racing, the more important it is to avoid weaving. Practice in a congested tune-up event, if possible.

---

6 TIPS FOR RACING IN A COSTUME[4]

It takes a special runner to complete a race in a wacky outfit— especially a race that doesn't explicitly encourage costumes. Dress up, and you'll delight spectators and fellow runners. (Well, maybe not the ones you're beating despite your sartorial challenges.) Here's how to enjoy being *that* weirdo at your next event.

1. **MAKE SURE YOUR RACE ALLOWS IT.** For security reasons, some races don't permit costumes or masks. If you can't find a policy on the website, contact the race director to make sure you're in the clear.

2. **LOOK INTO A GUINNESS WORLD RECORD.** If you're running a half or full marathon in costume, search the Guinness site to see if a mark has already been set for your distance, costume, and sex. You can apply to break an existing record or to set a new one—might as well, if you're racing in something uncomfortable anyway.

3. **DO A COUPLE PRACTICE RUNS.** You want to know before the big day whether to expect any random chafing, changes in your stride, or other problems. If you'd prefer not to run solo through your neighborhood in a Spider-Man suit, you can practice in a 5K or 10K race.

4. **USE ENOUGH LUBE.** Slather yourself in antichafing balm or petroleum jelly wherever the costume touches. For example, if your costume goes over your head, get your ears and under your chin.

5. **PREPARE TO BE THE CENTER OF ATTENTION.** If you're one of the few costumed runners in an otherwise normal race, everyone will notice you from start to finish. You'll hear spectators say, "Look, it's a (your costume)!" infinity times. Practice the smile-and-wave.

6. **BRING A HELPER.** If you are going for a Guinness record, you'll need photo evidence that you kept the costume on the whole way, and having someone else tote a camera and snap photos is easier than taking selfies. Plus, your sidekick can sign

a witness statement (also required for Guinness) and fetch you
water and gels.

6 STRATEGIES FOR RACING NAKED (THAT IS, WITHOUT ANY CLOTHES ON)[5]

When racing loses its adrenaline-pumping power, you might try an
obstacle race, a triathlon, or competing in a different sport entirely.
But you can make racing feel intimidating and challenging again
by running as nature intended: in your birthday suit. Most of us
aren't naked in public very often, except in our nightmares, so an
event that encourages nudity is likely well outside your comfort
zone. We consulted Selene Yeager—*Bicycling* magazine columnist,
fitness book author, and one-time naked duathlete—for tips for
first-timers to the nude-racing scene.

1. **PREPARE TO PANIC.** Yeager knew her race was set within
   the boundaries of a nudist resort, but she was still taken aback
   on race morning. "I pulled my car into registration and
   couldn't figure out what to do—everyone was already naked,
   and I still had my clothes on," Yeager says. "It was sort of
   reverse changing in the car: I just took off everything but my
   socks and running shoes and cap. It took all the nerve I had to
   get out."

2. **WAIT IT OUT.** The more time you spend in your sea of nudity,
   the less weird you'll feel.

3. **PREPARE TO BOUNCE.** "No matter who you are and what
   parts you have, something will be bouncing," Yeager says.
   Light, quick steps can help minimize the discomfort.

4. **INVEST IN STRONG SUNSCREEN.** The body parts that have
   never been exposed in public will need it the most.

5. **EMBRACE THE RIDICULOUSNESS.** You may be shirtless and
   pantsless, but you can still accessorize: "I wore tall rainbow
   socks and a bright green cap with bicycles on it," Yeager says.

6. **CARRY A TOWEL.** "You will want to sit down at some point,"

Yeager says. "You will not want to sit your bare nether regions on anything." The answer is a towel: Why rush to put your clothes back on when everyone's already seen you bouncing along the race course?

7 RACE-DAY TIPS FOR TRIATHLON NEWBIES[6]

Making the transition (yuk, yuk) from running races to a triathlon requires well-rounded fitness, additional training hours, and a more complex race plan. To help everything go smoothly when you try a tri, try the following.

1. **BUILD IN TIME.** Arrive even earlier than you would for a running race to prep your transition area, get marked with your number, and do a multisport warmup. Allot at least 90 minutes before go time.

2. **DO A REVERSE WARMUP.** Jog a bit first, then mount your bike for a short ride. Finish by getting into the water for a few practice strokes and, if it's chilly, to acclimate.

3. **LET EVERYONE GO.** Many first-time triathletes are most nervous about the chaos of the swim. If that's you, stand aside when the gun goes off, slowly count to five, and *then* begin. The small amount of time you'll lose beats wasting energy on panicking.

4. **SPOT WITHOUT SINKING.** About every five strokes during the swim, lift your gaze to make sure you're heading in the right direction. To make it easier, you can switch to breaststroke, but don't stop swimming—it's hard to regain momentum after treading water.

5. **CHANGE QUICKLY.** If you're wearing a wetsuit, you should start unzipping it as you run out of the water and finish removing it in the transition area. Dry your feet well, then put on your cycling shoes. Clip on your helmet, grab your bike, and run it to the course before hopping on.

6. **BIKE WISELY.** A common rookie mistake is hammering on the

bike, which fries your lower body before the run. Instead, maintain an effort level of seven out of 10. Use the bike leg as an opportunity to hydrate and, in longer races, refuel. It's the easiest time to eat and drink, if you practiced doing it in training (and you should have!).

7. **USE YOUR ARMS.** After you've transitioned to the run (your specialty!), your legs will likely feel a little sapped. It can help to focus on swinging your arms to help propel you forward, as they'll be relatively fresh postbike.

ACKNOWLEDGMENTS

I'D LIKE to thank my editors on this project, Mark Weinstein and Trisha de Guzman, for believing in a book with the word "poop" in the title and for their careful, thoughtful edits.

I'd also like to thank the many wonderful editors, writers, and experts I had the pleasure of working with during my 6 years at *Runner's World*. Special thanks to my longtime top editor, mentor, and running buddy Tish Hamilton, who helped me become a better journalist, thinker, and person, and to my online editor Chris Kraft, under whose leadership I was able to enjoy the thrill of "breaking a story" (Paul Ryan's "misremembered" marathon time) for the first time. I couldn't have written this book without the knowledge I amassed from assigning and editing training and racing stories at RW. And I wouldn't have enjoyed my time there nearly as much as I did without my #RunSquad, my lunch-run buddies, and everyone else livin' the dream in Emmaus and beyond.

Mom, thank you for always supporting me in my reading, writing, and running. This book *is* packaged for individual sale.

Paul, thank you for your patience as I've gotten progressively more (and blessedly less) obsessed with training for long-distance races. That period of obsession helped me write this book. It takes a special kind of partner to be shout-it-from-the-rooftops proud (instead of vaguely embarrassed) when his wife runs a marathon while dressed as a hot dog or writes a book called *How to Make Yourself Poop*. It's a good thing you're as much of a weirdo as I am.

REFERENCES

SECTION 1

1 Meghan Kita, "Easy Does It," *Runner's World*, accessed July 8, 2017, http://www.runnersworld.com/running-tips/easy-does-it.
2 Matt Fitzgerald, "Train at the Right Intensity Ratio," *Running Times*, accessed July 8, 2017, http://www.runnersworld.com/rt-web-exclusive/train-at-the-right-intensity-ratio.
3 Meghan Kita, "Easy Does It," *Runner's World*, accessed July 8, 2017, http://www.runnersworld.com/running-tips/easy-does-it.
4 Bob Cooper, "The 25 Golden Rules of Running," *Runner's World*, accessed July 8, 2017, http://www.runnersworld.com/running-tips/the-25-golden-rules-of-running/slide/2.
5 A. C. Shilton, "Master a Plan," *Runner's World*, September 2015, 38–40.
6 Ibid.
7 Ed Eyestone, "Making Your Long Runs Count," *Runner's World*, accessed July 8, 2017, http://www.runnersworld.com/race-training/making-your-long-runs-count.
8 Jenny Hadfield, "How to Run a Tempo Workout," *Runner's World*, accessed July 8, 2017, http://www.runnersworld.com/ask-coach-jenny/how-to-run-a-tempo-workout.
9 Scott Douglas, "Why Masters Runners Should Try Longer Training Cycles," *Runner's World*, accessed July 8, 2017, http://www.runnersworld.com/masters-training/why-masters-runners-should-try-longer-training-cycles.

CHAPTER 1

Cindy Kuzma, "Fair and Balanced," *Runner's World*, April 2015, 36–37.
Kelly Bastone, "This Is Not a Race," *Runner's World*, July 2015, 36–37.

3 Alex Hutchinson, "Minutes v. Miles," *Runner's World*, March 2013, 36.

4 Ibid.

5 Alex Hutchinson, "Formula for Success," *Runner's World*, January/February 2017, 46.

6 Cindy Kuzma, "Thrice as Nice," *Runner's World*, May 2016, 36–37.

7 Kelly Bastone, "Economic Gains," *Runner's World*, April 2016, 40–41.

8 Susan Paul, "Safety Tips for New Runners," *Runner's World*, accessed July 8, 2017, http://www.runnersworld.com/for-beginners-only/safety-tips-for-new -runners.

9 "Light the Way," *Runner's World*, January/February 2017, 37.

10 Susan Paul, "Safety Tips for New Runners," *Runner's World*, accessed July 8, 2017, http://www.runnersworld.com/for-beginners-only/safety-tips-for-new -runners.

11 "What to Do If You're Attacked by a Dog," *Runner's World*, accessed July 8, 2017, http://www.runnersworld.com/running-tips/what-to-do-if-youre -attacked-by-a-dog.

12 Kelly Bastone, "Levels of Difficulty," *Runner's World*, October 2015, 34–37.

13 Jeff Galloway, "Trail Running for Beginners," *Runner's World*, accessed July 12, 2017, http://www.runnersworld.com/trail-running/trail-running-for -beginners.

14 A. C. Shilton, "Master a Plan," *Runner's World*, September 2015, 38–40.

15 Bob Cooper, "Getaway Plans," *Runner's World*, June 2014, 25–26.

16 A. C. Shilton, "Stay Fit and Kick Back," *Runner's World*, July 2016, 36–38.

CHAPTER 2

1 Amanda MacMillan, "How to Make Yourself Poop," *Runner's World*, accessed July 8, 2017, http://www.runnersworld.com/health/how-to-make-yourself -poop.

2 Enrique Rivero, "Suffering from Constipation? Self-Acupressure Can Help," UCLA Newsroom, accessed July 8, 2017, http://newsroom.ucla.edu/releases /suffering-from-constipation.

3 Jennifer Van Allen, "How and Why You Should Warm Up before a Run," *Runner's World*, accessed July 8, 2017, http://www.runnersworld.com /run-nonstop/how-and-why-you-should-warm-up-before-a-run.

CHAPTER 3

1 Jenny Hadfield, "Ditch the Stitch," *Runner's World*, March 2014, 42.

2 Ibid.

3 "Midrun Mishaps," *Runner's World*, June 2009, 46.

4 Ibid.

5 Jeff Galloway, "Go! Then Slow! Then Go," *Runner's World*, January/February 2015, 38.

6 Ibid.

7 Alex Hutchinson, "Recover Right," *Runner's World*, March 2014, 28.

8 Ibid.

9 Gigi Douban, "Afraid to Ask," *Runner's World*, May 2008, 54.

10 Matthew Solan, "School of Walk," *Runner's World*, December 2013, 35–36.

11 Ibid.

12 Kelly Bastone, "Levels of Difficulty," *Runner's World*, October 2015, 34–37.

13 Jenny Hadfield, "Ditch the Stitch," *Runner's World*, March 2014, 42.

14 Jeff Galloway, "Miles of Smiles," *Runner's World*, March 2015, 38.

15 Cindy Kuzma, "5 Ways for Women to (Discreetly) Pee in Public," *Runner's World*, accessed July 8, 2017, http://www.runnersworld.com/running-tips /5-ways-for-women-to-discreetly-pee-in-public.

16 Dimity McDowell, "Weird Science," *Runner's World*, September 2010, 72–80.

17 Gigi Douban, "Afraid to Ask," *Runner's World*, May 2008, 54.

CHAPTER 4

1 Jennifer Van Allen, "5 Speed Workouts Every New Runner Should Try," *Runner's World*, accessed July 8, 2017, http://www.runnersworld.com /run-faster/5-speed-workouts-every-new-runner-should-try.

2 Phil Latter, "Speed Play," *Runner's World*, accessed July 8, 2017, http://www .runnersworld.com/running-tips/speed-play.

3 Ibid.

4 Alex Hutchinson, "How Unstructured Runs Can Make You Faster," *Runner's World*, accessed July 8, 2017, http://www.runnersworld.com/the-fast-lane /how-unstructured-runs-can-make-you-faster.

5 Pete Rea, "The Super Six Workouts," *Running Times*, accessed July 8, 2017, http://www.runnersworld.com/workouts/the-super-six-workouts.

6 "Intervals," *Runner's World*, accessed July 8, 2017, http://www.runnersworld .com/tag/intervals.

7 Greg MacMillan, "Stamina and Speed Quarters," *Running Times*, accessed July 8, 2017, http://www.runnersworld.com/workouts/stamina-and-speed -quarters.

8 Alex Hutchinson, "Extra Reps," *Runner's World*, May 2017, 26–27.

9 "Yasso 800s," *Runner's World*, accessed July 8, 2017, http://www .runnersworld.com/tag/yasso-800s.

10 Ibid.

11 Michelle Hamilton, "Magic Mile Repeats," *Runner's World*, accessed July 8, 2017, http://www.runnersworld.com/workouts/magic-mile-repeats.

12 "Ask the Experts," *Runner's World*, July 2014, 34.

13 Cindy Kuzma, "Start Hard, Finish Easy," *Runner's World*, accessed July 8, 2017, http://www.runnersworld.com/race-training/start-hard-finish-easy.

14 The *Runner's World* Editors, "How Many Miles Is a 5K?" *Runner's World*, accessed July 8, 2017, http://www.runnersworld.com/races/how-many-miles -is-a-5k.

15 "Episode 50: How to Train Your Best," *Runner's World*, accessed July 8, 2017, http://www.runnersworld.com/the-runners-world-show/episode-50-how-to -train-your-best.

16 Ibid.

17 Cindy Kuzma, "Speed for All," *Runner's World*, October 2016, 32–33.

18 Alex Hutchinson, "Recover Right," *Runner's World*, March 2014, 28.

19 Cindy Kuzma, "Full Tilt," *Runner's World*, April 2013, 33–34.

20 Ibid.

21 Ibid.

22 Ibid.

23 Jordan Metzl, MD, "HIIT Plan," *Runner's World*, January/February 2017, 58–59.

24 Hal Higdon, "Zoom, Zoom," *Runner's World*, April 2017, 38.

25 Karen Asp, "Tempo Runs Increase Speed and Endurance," *Runner's World*, accessed July 8, 2017, http://www.runnersworld.com/running-tips/tempo -runs-increase-speed-and-endurance.

26   Scott Douglas, "The Fast Break," *Runner's World*, March 2017, 33.
27   Lisa Marshall, "Out of Gas? Don't Stop," *Runner's World*, July 2016, 44.

CHAPTER 5

1   Adam Buckley Cohen, "For the Long Haul," *Runner's World*, October 2014, 42–43.
2   Cindy Kuzma, "How to Do a Long Run and Still Be Able to Get Off the Couch Later," *Runner's World*, accessed July 8, 2017, http://www.runnersworld.com /fatigue/how-to-do-a-long-run-and-still-be-able-to-get-off-the-couch-later.
3   Jessica Migala, "Whine and Shine," *Runner's World*, November 2015, 42–43.
4   Ibid.

CHAPTER 6

1   John Hanc, "So Inclined," *Runner's World*, July 2010, 27–30.
2   Mario Fraioli, "Hit the Hills," *Running Times*, accessed July 8, 2017, http://www.runnersworld.com/race-training/hit-the-hills.
3   John Hanc, "So Inclined," *Runner's World*, July 2010, 27–30.
4   Jeff Galloway, "On the Up Side," *Runner's World*, September 2012, 38.
5   Jenny Hadfield, "How to Learn to Love Running Hills," *Runner's World*, accessed July 8, 2017, http://www.runnersworld.com/ask-coach-jenny /how-to-learn-to-love-running-hills.
6   John Hanc, "So Inclined," *Runner's World*, July 2010, 27–30.
7   Ibid.
8   Cindy Kuzma, "Down You Go," *Runner's World*, May 2014, 35–36.
9   Jeff Galloway, "On the Up Side," *Runner's World*, September 2012, 38.
10   Matthew Solan, "Step It Up," *Runner's World*, February 2014, 26.
11   Ibid.
12   Alicia Shay, e-mail to author, February 4, 2014.
13   Kelly Bastone, "Levels of Difficulty," *Runner's World*, October 2015, 34–37.

CHAPTER 7

1   A. C. Shilton, "Stay Fit and Kick Back," *Runner's World*, July 2016, 36–38.
2   Jeff Galloway, "Survive a Scorcher," *Runner's World*, August 2016, 44.
3   Kristen Dold, "Take the Plunge," *Runner's World*, August 2017, 14–17.
4   "Ask the Experts," *Runner's World*, August 2016, 52.
5   Alex Hutchinson, "Sweat It," *Runner's World*, June 2015, 42.
6   A. C. Shilton, "Sweat to Succeed," *Runner's World*, December 2016, 40.
7   Jeff Galloway, "Work Out Winter," *Runner's World*, January 2014, 26.
8   Doug Most, "Rise & Run," *Runner's World*, October 2011, 50–55.
9   Cindy Kuzma, "Stay Safe on the Treadmill," *Runner's World*, accessed July 8, 2017, http://www.runnersworld.com/newswire/stay-safe-on-the-treadmill.

CHAPTER 8

1   Caitlin Carlson, "See the Future," *Runner's World*, October 2016, 40.
2   A. C. Shilton, "Plan of Cutback," *Runner's World*, November 2015, 48.
3   Cindy Kuzma, "Golden Opportunity," *Runner's World*, November 2014, 34–35.
4   Caitlin Carlson, "Between the Lines," *Runner's World*, June 2016, 42.
5   Cindy Kuzma, "The Relay Way," *Runner's World*, August 2013, 27–28.
6   Ali Nolan, "4 Workouts That Get You Ready for an Obstacle Course Race,"

Runner's World, accessed July 8, 2017, http://www.runnersworld.com
/workouts/4-workouts-that-get-you-ready-for-an-obstacle-course-race.

SECTION 2

1   Liz Applegate, "The New Rules of Food," *Runner's World*, accessed July 8,
    2017, http://www.runnersworld.com/nutrition/the-new-rules-of-food.
2   Danielle Zickl , "Eat like an Elite: Chris Mosier," *Runner's World*, accessed
    July 8, 2017, http://www.runnersworld.com/eat-like-an-elite/eat-like-an
    -elite-chris-mosier.
3   Alicia Shay, e-mail to author, February 4, 2014.
4   Dimity McDowell, "8 Hydration Myths Busted," *Runner's World*, accessed
    July 8, 2017, http://www.runnersworld.com/hydration-dehydration
    /8-hydration-myths-busted.
5   Ibid.
6   Pamela Nisevich Bede, "6 Rules for Eating Right as a Runner," *Runner's World*,
    accessed July 8, 2017, http://www.runnersworld.com/start-running/6-rules
    -for-eating-right-as-a-runner.
7   Sarah Bowen Shea, "Carbs on the Run," *Runner's World*, accessed July 8, 2017,
    http://www.runnersworld.com/nutrition/fuel-for-a-runners-diet.
8   Bob Cooper, "The 25 Golden Rules of Running," *Runner's World*, accessed July
    8, 2017, http://www.runnersworld.com/running-tips/the-25-golden-rules-of
    -running.

CHAPTER 9

1   Dimity McDowell, "8 Hydration Myths Busted," *Runner's World*, accessed
    July 8, 2017, http://www.runnersworld.com/hydration-dehydration
    /8-hydration-myths-busted.
2   Selene Yeager, "Race-Day Disasters," *Runner's World*, October 2012, 63–68.
3   "Hyponatremia," *Runner's World*, accessed July 8, 2017, http://www
    .runnersworld.com/tag/hyponatremia.
4   Dimity McDowell, "Fluid Facts," *Runner's World*, August 2013, 37–38.
5   Liz Applegate, "Good News," *Runner's World*, October 2013, 44.
6   "Ask a Nutritionist," *Runner's World*, August 2015, 100.
7   "Ask the Experts," *Runner's World*, July 2008, 40.
8   Dimity McDowell, "Fluid Facts," *Runner's World*, August 2013, 37–38.
9   "Hyponatremia," *Runner's World*, accessed July 8, 2017, http://www
    .runnersworld.com/tag/hyponatremia.
10 Pamela Nisevich Bede, "16 Healthy (and Yummy) Prerun Meals and Snacks,"
    Runner's World, accessed July 8, 2017, http://www.runnersworld.com
    /run-longer/16-healthy-and-yummy-prerun-meals-and-snacks.
11 Liz Applegate, "Fill'r Up," *Runner's World*, May 2011, 48.
12 Melissa Wagenberg, "Road Food," *Runner's World*, June 2009, 36–37.
13 USDA Food Composition Databases, accessed September 25, 2017, https://ndb
    .nal.usda.gov/ndb.
14 "Staffer Stashes," *Runner's World*, August 2015, 60.
15 Pamela Nisevich Bede, "How to Keep Fuel from Freezing in Winter," *Runner's
    World*, accessed July 8, 2017, http://www.runnersworld.com/fuel-school
    /how-to-keep-fuel-from-freezing-in-winter.
16 USDA Food Composition Databases, accessed July 22, 2017, https://ndb.nal
    .usda.gov/ndb.

17 Liz Applegate, "Fill'r Up," *Runner's World*, May 2011, 48.

18 Ibid.

19 Ibid.

20 Cindy Kuzma, "26.2 for You," *Runner's World*, July 2016, 83–89.

21 USDA Food Composition Databases, accessed July 22, 2017, https://ndb.nal
    .usda.gov/ndb.

22 USDA Food Composition Databases, accessed July 22, 2017, https://ndb.nal
    .usda.gov/ndb.

23 Bob Cooper, "The 25 Golden Rules of Running," *Runner's World*, accessed
    July 8, 2017, http://www.runnersworld.com/running-tips/the-25-golden
    -rules-of-running.

24 Pamela Nisevich Bede, "Is Chocolate Milk Really Best for Recovery?"
    Runner's World, accessed July 8, 2017, http://www.runnersworld.com/fuel
    -school/is-chocolate-milk-really-best-for-recovery.

25 Dimity McDowell, "The Right Way to Carbo-Load before a Race," *Runner's
    World*, accessed July 8, 2017, http://www.runnersworld.com/nutrition/the
    -right-way-to-carbo-load-before-a-race.

26 Leslie Bonci, "Carbo Loading without Exploding," *Runner's World*, accessed
    July 8, 2017, http://www.runnersworld.com/ask-the-sports-dietitian/carbo
    -loading-without-exploding.

27 Dimity McDowell, "The Right Way to Carbo-Load before a Race," *Runner's
    World*, accessed July 8, 2017, http://www.runnersworld.com/nutrition/the
    -right-way-to-carbo-load-before-a-race.

28 Ibid.

29 Ibid.

30 Ibid.

31 Ibid.

32 Liz Applegate, "Belly Aching," *Runner's World*, April 2014, 36.

33 Megan Hetzel, "5 Reasons That Running Can Make You Puke," *Runner's
    World*, accessed July 8, 2017, http://www.runnersworld.com/health
    /5-reasons-that-running-can-make-you-puke.

34 Liz Applegate, "Chug-Run Conundrum," *Runner's World*, August 2016, 56.

CHAPTER 10

1 Liz Applegate, "Feast First," *Runner's World*, January/February 2017, 56.

2 Liz Applegate, "Coffee Perks," *Runner's World*, March 2014, 34.

3 The *Runner's World* Editors, "25 Great Snacks for Runners," *Runner's World*,
   accessed July 8, 2017, http://www.runnersworld.com/snacks/25-great-snacks
   -for-runners.

4 Amanda MacMillan, "Not So Innocent," *Runner's World*, October 2015, 44.

5 Heather Mayer Irvine, "Deceptively Sweet," *Runner's World*, April 2016, 50–51.

6 Michelle Hamilton, "Your Brain Isn't Fooled by Artificial Sweeteners,"
   Runner's World, accessed July 8, 2017, http://www.runnersworld.com
   /newswire/your-brain-isnt-fooled-by-artificial-sweeteners.

7 Jennifer Van Allen, "Kick Your Sugar Addiction in 9 Steps," *Runner's World*,
   accessed July 8, 2017, http://www.runnersworld.com/run-faster/kick-your
   -sugar-addiction-in-9-steps.

8 Robert M. Califf, MD, and Susan Mayne, PhD, "Unveiling the New Nutrition
   Facts Label," US Food and Drug Administration, accessed July 8, 2017,
   https://blogs.fda.gov/fdavoice/index.php/2016/05/unveiling-the-new
   -nutrition-facts-label.

9   Amy Gorin, MS, RDN, "More Power to You," *Runner's World*, September 2016, 46–48.

10 Jackie Dikos, RD, "A Runner's Guide to Becoming a Vegetarian," *Running Times*, accessed July 8, 2017, http://www.runnersworld.com/rt-web-exclusive /a-runners-guide-to-becoming-a-vegetarian.

11 Jessica Migala, "Nosh at Night," *Runner's World*, May 2015, 54.

CHAPTER 11

1   Cindy Kuzma, "Hop on the Habit Trail," *Runner's World*, January/February 2015, 64–72.

2   Stephanie Eckelkamp, "5 Things I Learned from a Month of Meal-Prepping," *Runner's World*, accessed July 8, 2017, http://www.runnersworld.com/recipes /5-things-i-learned-from-a-month-of-meal-prepping.

3   Cindy Kuzma, "18 Household Items Runners Should Toss—And 5 to Keep," *Runner's World*, accessed July 8, 2017, http://www.runnersworld.com /health/18-household-items-runners-should-toss-and-5-to-keep.

CHAPTER 12

1   Kelly Bastone, "Start Where You Are," *Runner's World*, January/February 2017, 66–80.

2   Amby Burfoot, "A Weight-Loss Manifesto," *Runner's World*, April 2015, 60–65.

3   Liz Applegate, "A Fresh Way to Lose," *Runner's World*, January/February 2015, 46–47.

4   Denise Schipani, "Weighty Errors," *Runner's World*, January 2014, 32–34.

5   Kelly Bastone, "You're Really Eating That?" *Runner's World*, January/ February 2016, 50–52.

6   Matthew Kadey, "Messy Eater," *Runner's World*, July 2016, 50–52.

7   A. C. Shilton, "Fat Chance!" *Runner's World*, December 2015, 82–86.

8   Sarah Bowen Shea, "Carbs on the Run," *Runner's World*, September 2008, 39–40.

9   Ibid.

10 A. C. Shilton, "Fat Chance!" *Runner's World*, December 2015, 82–86.

11 Matthew Kadey, MS, RD, "Incredible Weight Loss Myths Exposed!" *Runner's World*, April 2010, 56–66.

12 Ibid.

13 A. C. Shilton, "Fat Chance!" *Runner's World*, December 2015, 82–86.

14 Liz Applegate, "Power Plants," *Runner's World*, August 2000, 32–34.

15 Bob Cooper, "Something Old, Something New," *Runner's World*, November 2016, 78–81.

16 Liz Applegate, "A Fresh Way to Lose," *Runner's World*, January/February 2015, 46–47.

SECTION 3

1   Jennifer Van Allen, "How to Buy Running Shoes," *Runner's World*, accessed July 8, 2017, http://www.runnersworld.com/start-walking/how-to-buy -running-shoes.

2   Scott Douglas, "Study Backs Rotating Shoes to Lower Injury Risk," *Runner's World*, accessed July 8, 2017, http://www.runnersworld.com/newswire/study -backs-rotating-shoes-to-lower-injury-risk.

3   Jennifer Van Allen, "How to Buy Running Shoes," *Runner's World*, accessed July 8, 2017, http://www.runnersworld.com/start-walking/how-to-buy-running-shoes.

4   "Running Shoe FAQ," *Runner's World*, accessed July 8, 2017, http://www.runnersworld.com/running-shoes/running-shoe-questions.

5   Bob Cooper, "The 25 Golden Rules of Running," *Runner's World*, accessed July 8, 2017, http://www.runnersworld.com/running-tips/the-25-golden-rules-of-running.

6   Yishane Lee, "The Pack Rules: Save Big Money," *Runner's World*, accessed July 8, 2017, http://www.runnersworld.com/running-tips/how-to-save-money-when-running.

7   Sarah Lorge Butler, "25 Tricks for Saving Money on Your Running in 2017," *Runner's World*, accessed July 8, 2017, http://www.runnersworld.com/general-interest/25-tricks-for-saving-money-on-your-running-in-2017.

CHAPTER 13

1   The Runner's World Editors, "Gear Tip: How to Tie Your Shoes," *Runner's World,* accessed July 8, 2017, http://www.runnersworld.com/gear-tip/gear-tip-how-to-tie-your-shoes.

2   Susan Rinkunas, "Alternative Ways to Tie Your Running Shoes," *Runner's World,* accessed July 8, 2017, http://www.runnersworld.com/running-tips/alternative-ways-to-tie-your-running-shoes.

3   Jeff Dengate, "Gear Tip: Liner Notes," *Runner's World,* accessed July 8, 2017, http://www.runnersworld.com/gear-tip/gear-tip-liner-notes.

4   The Runner's World Editors, "Take the Wet Test: Learn Your Foot Type," *Runner's World,* accessed July 8, 2017, http://www.runnersworld.com/running-shoes/the-wet-test.

5   Alex Hutchinson, "How Much Do Heavy Shoes Slow You Down?," *Runner's World,* accessed July 8, 2017, http://www.runnersworld.com/sweat-science/how-much-do-heavy-shoes-slow-you-down.

CHAPTER 14

1   Valerie Moyer, "Stop the Stink," *Running Times*, accessed July 8, 2017, http://www.runnersworld.com/other-gear/stop-the-stink.

2   Jeff Dengate, "Beating the Heat," *Runner's World*, accessed July 8, 2017, http://www.runnersworld.com/rw-vip-editor-blogs/beating-the-heat.

3   Steve Rushin, "From Barefoot to Fitbit," *Runner's World*, accessed July 8, 2017, http://www.runnersworld.com/50th-anniversary/from-barefoot-to-fitbit.

4   Scott Douglas, "Synthetic Workout Gear Smells Worse Than Cotton Gear," *Runner's World*, accessed July 8, 2017, http://www.runnersworld.com/newswire/synthetic-workout-gear-smells-worse-than-cotton-gear.

5   Valerie Moyer, "Stop the Stink," *Running Times*, accessed July 8, 2017, http://www.runnersworld.com/other-gear/stop-the-stink.

6   Jeff Galloway, "Still Going Strong," *Runner's World*, November 2016, 42.

7   Jeff Dengate, "Gear Tip: Store Mid-Run Fuel," *Runner's World*, accessed July 8, 2017, http://www.runnersworld.com/gear-tip/gear-tip-easy-ways-to-store-mid-run-fuel.

8   Katie Neitz, "How to Find the Proper Sports Bra," *Runner's World*, accessed July 8, 2017, http://www.runnersworld.com/shoes-gear-video/how-to-find-the-proper-sports-bra.

9   "Compression," *Runner's World*, accessed July 8, 2017, http://www
    .runnersworld.com/tag/compression.
10 Chris Dickey, e-mail to author, June 5, 2017.

CHAPTER 15

1   Kelly Bastone, "The Trouble with Cheap Treadmills," *Runner's World*,
    accessed July 8, 2017, http://www.runnersworld.com/treadmills/the-trouble
    -with-cheap-treadmills.
2   Nicole Collins, "Buying a Used Treadmill," *Runner's World*, accessed July 8,
    2017, http://www.runnersworld.com/other-gear/how-to-buy-a-used
    -treadmill.
3   Shanna Burnette, "An Athlete's Guide to Running Strollers," *Running Times*,
    accessed July 8, 2017, http://www.runnersworld.com/running-gear/an
    -athletes-guide-to-running-strollers.
4   Jenny Hadfield, "How to Shop for a Budget-Friendly Running Stroller,"
    Runner's World, accessed July 8, 2017, http://www.runnersworld.com/ask
    -coach-jenny/how-to-shop-for-a-budget-friendly-running-stroller.
5   Jeff Dengate, "Gear Tip: Properly Wrap Your Headphones," *Runner's World*,
    accessed July 8, 2017, http://www.runnersworld.com/gear-tip/gear-tip
    -properly-wrap-your-headphones.

CHAPTER 16

1   "Ask RW," *Runner's World*, June 2017, 43–45.
2   Cindy Kuzma, "10 Things Your Dermatologist Really Wishes You Wouldn't
    Do," *Runner's World*, accessed July 8, 2017, http://www.runnersworld.com
    /health/10-things-your-dermatologist-really-wishes-you-wouldnt-do.
3   Shirley Dang, "How to Choose the Best Sunglasses," American Academy of
    Ophthalmology, accessed July 8, 2017, https://www.aao.org/eye-health
    /tips-prevention/top-sunglasses-tips.
4   Sarah Lorge Butler, "Run and Sun: Protect Your Skin," *Running Times*,
    accessed July 8, 2017, http://www.runnersworld.com/injury-prevention
    -recovery/run-and-sun-protect-your-skin.
5   Cindy Kuzma, "Hop on the Habit Trail," *Runner's World*, January/February
    2015, 64–72.
6   Cindy Kuzma, "10 Things Your Dermatologist Really Wishes You Wouldn't
    Do," *Runner's World*, accessed July 8, 2017, http://www.runnersworld.com
    /health/10-things-your-dermatologist-really-wishes-you-wouldnt-do.
7   Sarah Lorge Butler, "Run and Sun: Protect Your Skin," *Running Times*,
    accessed July 8, 2017, http://www.runnersworld.com/injury-prevention
    -recovery/run-and-sun-protect-your-skin.
8   Ibid.
9   Blane Bachelor, "Pure Friction," *Runner's World*, July 2015, 58.
10 Heather Johnson, "You Run: Your Makeup Should Not," *Runner's World*,
    accessed July 8, 2017, http://www.runnersworld.com/run-matters/you-run
    -your-makeup-should-not.
11 Ibid.
12 Cindy Kuzma, "Can Foam Rolling Give You a Mental Boost?" *Runner's World*,
    accessed July 8, 2017, http://www.runnersworld.com/foam-roller/can-foam
    -rolling-give-you-a-mental-boost.

13   Meghan Rabbitt, "5 Different Types of Foam Rollers—and When to Use Each One," *Runner's World*, accessed July 8, 2017, http://www.runnersworld.com /foam-roller/5-types-of-foam-rollers.

14   Ibid.

15   Ibid.

16   Caitlin Chock, "Self-Massage the Runner's Way," *Running Times*, accessed July 8, 2017, http://www.runnersworld.com/injury-prevention-recovery /self-massage-the-runners-way.

17   Cindy Kuzma, "What Runners Need to Know about Menstrual Cups," *Runner's World*, accessed July 8, 2017, http://www.runnersworld.com/run -matters/what-runners-need-to-know-about-menstrual-cups.

18   Caitlin Chock, "Self-Massage the Runner's Way," *Running Times*, accessed July 8, 2017, http://www.runnersworld.com/injury-prevention-recovery /self-massage-the-runners-way.

19   Jeff Dengate, "6 Products for Recovery from Running," *Runner's World*, accessed July 8, 2017, http://www.runnersworld.com/injury-prevention -recovery/6-products-for-recovery-from-running.

20   David Alm, "How to Keep Your Junk in Your Shorts," *Runner's World*, accessed July 8, 2017, http://www.runnersworld.com/general-interest /how-to-keep-your-junk-in-your-shorts.

CHAPTER 17

1   Jenny Hadfield, "How to Dress for Rainy Runs," *Runner's World*, accessed July 8, 2017, http://www.runnersworld.com/ask-coach-jenny/how-to-dress -for-rainy-runs.

2   "Make Your Gear Last," *Runner's World*, accessed July 8, 2017, http://www .runnersworld.com/running-shoes/make-your-gear-last.

3   Susan Paul, "The Newbie Guide to Running When It's Cold," *Runner's World*, accessed July 8, 2017, http://www.runnersworld.com/for-beginners-only /the-newbie-guide-to-running-when-its-cold.

4   Lisa Jhung, "Trail Ready," *Runner's World*, October 2015, 60.

5   Bryan Boyle, "Ask the Gear Guy: Do I Need Specific Shoes for Trail Running?" *Runner's World*, accessed July 8, 2017, http://www.runnersworld.com/gear -check/ask-the-gear-guy-do-i-need-specific-shoes-for-trail-running.

CHAPTER 18

1   Cindy Kuzma, "18 Household Items Runners Should Toss—And 5 to Keep," *Runner's World*, accessed July 8, 2017, http://www.runnersworld.com /health/18-household-items-runners-should-toss-and-5-to-keep.

2   Kelly Bastone, "Find Your Spark," *Runner's World*, December 2016, 34–35.

CHAPTER 19

1   Jenny Hadfield, "12 Ways to Get Out of a Running Rut," *Runner's World*, accessed July 8, 2017, http://www.runnersworld.com/ask-coach-jenny /12-ways-to-get-out-of-a-running-rut.

2   Jeff Galloway, "The Running Dead," *Runner's World*, September 2015, 42.

3   Dimity McDowell, "Run and Retweet," *Runner's World*, September 2013, 72–73.

4   Des Linden, @des_linden Twitter feed, accessed July 20, 2017, https://twitter .com/des_linden/status/839101307134816256.

5   Dimity McDowell, "Run and Retweet," *Runner's World*, September 2013, 72–73.

6   Yishane Lee, "The Pack Rules: Your Best Tips," *Runner's World*, December 2011, 70–71.

7   Ibid.

8   Beth Dreher, "Get Over It," *Runner's World*, accessed July 8, 2017, http://www.runnersworld.com/running-tips/overcome-common-running-obstacles.

9   Alex Hutchinson, "1 Hour of Running Adds 7 Hours of Life," *Runner's World*, accessed July 8, 2017, http://www.runnersworld.com/health-injuries/1-hour-of-running-adds-7-hours-of-life.

CHAPTER 20

1   Yishane Lee, "The Pack Rules: Tough It Out," *Runner's World*, accessed July 8, 2017, http://www.runnersworld.com/runners-stories/tips-for-toughing-it-out-on-a-run.

2   Alex Hutchinson, "Talk Yourself Up," *Runner's World*, June 2017, 26–27.

3   Dimity McDowell, "Run and Retweet," *Runner's World*, September 2013, 72–73.

4   Christie Aschwanden, "The Magic of Mantras," *Runner's World*, February 2011, 56–59.

5   Ibid.

6   Dimity McDowell, "Run and Retweet," *Runner's World*, September 2013, 72–73.

7   Christie Aschwanden, "The Magic of Mantras," *Runner's World*, February 2011, 56–59.

8   Jenny Hadfield, "How to Run Long on the Treadmill without Losing Your Mind," *Runner's World*, accessed July 8, 2017, http://www.runnersworld.com/ask-coach-jenny/how-to-run-long-on-the-treadmill-without-losing-your-mind.

9   Gigi Douban, "Power of One," *Runner's World*, March 2015, 56.

10 Jeff Galloway, "A Natural High," *Runner's World*, July 2016, 40.

11 K. Aleisha Fetters, "How to Achieve a Runner's High," *Runner's World*, accessed July 8, 2017, http://www.runnersworld.com/running-tips/how-to-achieve-a-runners-high.

CHAPTER 21

1   Nicole Ginley-Hidinger, "How to Find a Team Using the Find a Runner Tool," Ragnar, accessed July 8, 2017, https://www.runragnar.com/ragnar-road-blog/2016/05/find-team-using-find-runner-tool.

2   Scott Douglas, "The Effects of Music Before, During and After Running," *Runner's World*, accessed July 8, 2017, http://www.runnersworld.com/newswire/the-effects-of-music-before-during-and-after-running.

3   Songbpm.com, accessed July 20, 2017, https://songbpm.com/bruce-springsteen/born-to-run.

4   Scott Douglas, "The Effects of Music Before, During and After Running," *Runner's World*, accessed July 8, 2017, http://www.runnersworld.com/newswire/the-effects-of-music-before-during-and-after-running.

5   Lauren Bedosky, "It's Science!" *Runner's World*, August 2016, 42–43.

6   Ibid.

7   "Running Songs," Jog.fm, accessed July 20, 2017, https://jog.fm/workout-songs.

8   Jennifer Van Allen, "Mars & Venus on the Run," *Runner's World,* June 2013, 70–76.

9   Nick Trout, "Make Your Dog Your Running Partner," *Runner's World,* accessed July 8, 2017, http://www.runnersworld.com/running-with-dogs /make-your-dog-your-running-partner.

CHAPTER 22

1   Meghan G. Loftus, "Yes, Coach?" *Runner's World,* July 2015, 66–76.

2   Sarah Lorge Butler, "25 Tricks for Saving Money on Your Running in 2017," *Runner's World,* accessed July 8, 2017, http://www.runnersworld.com /general-interest/25-tricks-for-saving-money-on-your-running-in-2017.

3   Nicole Falcone, "Destination: Race!" *Runner's World,* June 2012, 58–64.

4   Jenny Hadfield, "Runners and Blood Clots: What You Need to Know," *Runner's World,* accessed July 8, 2017, http://www.runnersworld.com/ask -coach-jenny/runners-and-blood-clots-what-you-need-to-know.

CHAPTER 23

1   Meghan Kita, "Year in Review," *Runner's World,* accessed July 8, 2017, http://www.runnersworld.com/running-tips/learn-from-your-running-log.

2   Kelly Bastone, "Start Where You Are," *Runner's World,* January/February 2017, 66–80.

3   Meghan Kita and Jenny McCoy, "Magic Bullets," *Runner's World,* May 2017, 56–61.

4   Jeff Galloway, "If They Can't Say Something Nice . . . " *Runner's World,* August 2017, 29.

5   Kelly Bastone, "Let It Flow," *Runner's World,* April 2016, 56–59.

6   Ibid.

7   Amanda Tust, "Forward Thinker," *Runner's World,* January 2014, 44.

SECTION 5

1   Amby Burfoot, "The 10 Laws of Injury Prevention," *Runner's World,* accessed July 22, 2017, http://www.runnersworld.com/health/the-10-laws-of-injury -prevention.

2   Amby Burfoot, "Amby Burfoot's Simple Secrets to a Lifetime of Running," *Runner's World,* accessed July 22, 2017, http://www.runnersworld.com /runners-stories/amby-burfoots-simple-secrets-to-a-lifetime-of-running.

3   Bob Cooper, "The 25 Golden Rules of Running," *Runner's World,* accessed July 22, 2017, http://www.runnersworld.com/running-tips/the-25-golden-rules -of-running.

CHAPTER 24

1   Jeff Galloway, "Ground Advice," *Runner's World,* April 2015, 40.

2   http://www.runnersworld.com/health/the-10-laws-of-injury-prevention, March 2010.

3   Ed Eyestone, "Hit Your Marks," *Runner's World,* April 2011, 40.

4   A. C. Shilton, "Oh, Cramp!" *Runner's World,* November 2014, 52–54.

5   Ibid.

6   Tom Layman, "5 Things Your Sports Chiropractor Wishes You Would Stop Doing," *Runner's World,* accessed July 22, 2017, http://www.runnersworld

.com/injury-prevention/5-things-your-sports-chiropractor-wishes-you
-would-stop-doing.

7   Jenny Hadfield, "How to Prevent Nipple Chafing," *Runner's World*, accessed
     July 22, 2017, http://www.runnersworld.com/ask-coach-jenny/how-to
     -prevent-nipple-chafing.

8   Gretchen Voss, "Ticked Off!" *Runner's World*, July 2014, 76–83.

9   "Permethrin: General Fact Sheet," National Pesticide Information Center,
     accessed July 22, 2017, http://npic.orst.edu/factsheets/PermGen.html.

10   Gretchen Voss, "Ticked Off!" *Runner's World*, July 2014, 76–83.

CHAPTER 25

1   Alex Hutchinson and Meghan Kita, "Do You Stretch after Running?" *Runner's
     World*, accessed July 22, 2017, http://www.runnersworld.com/running
     -debates/do-you-stretch-after-running.

2   Katie Neitz, "Unknot Yourself," *Runner's World*, October 2015, 56–58.

3   Susan Paul, "7 Ways to Fix Your Postrun Recovery," *Runner's World*, accessed
     July 22, 2017, http://www.runnersworld.com/for-beginners-only/7-ways-to
     -fix-your-postrun-recovery.

4   Cindy Kuzma, "Can Foam Rolling Give You a Mental Boost?" *Runner's World*,
     accessed July 22, 2017, http://www.runnersworld.com/foam-roller/can-foam
     -rolling-give-you-a-mental-boost.

5   Michelle Hamilton, "How to Use a Foam Roller," *Runner's World*, accessed
     July 22, 2017, http://www.runnersworld.com/foam-roller/how-to-use-a-foam
     -roller.

6   Jenny McCoy and Carl Leivers, "Foam Rolling? Do It Right by Avoiding These
     10 Mistakes," *Runner's World*, accessed July 22, 2017, http://www
     .runnersworld.com/injury-prevention-recovery/foam-rolling-do-it-right-by
     -avoiding-these-10-mistakes.

7   Scott Douglas, "Two Studies Back Benefits of Ice Baths," *Runner's World*,
     accessed July 22, 2017, http://www.runnersworld.com/newswire/two
     -studies-back-benefits-of-ice-baths.

8   Nikki Kimball, "Ice Baths: Cold Therapy," *Runner's World*, accessed July 22, 2017,
     http://www.runnersworld.com/health/the-benefits-of-ice-baths-for-runners.

9   Ibid.

10   Kristin Barry, "The Most Effective Way to Use Down Weeks," *Running Times*,
     accessed July 22, 2017, http://www.runnersworld.com/race-training/the
     -most-effective-way-to-use-down-weeks.

11   Bradley Stulberg, "Positively Healthy," *Runner's World*, June 2016, 54–56.

12   Cindy Kuzma, "How to Get Better Sleep as a Runner," *Runner's World*,
     accessed July 22, 2017, http://www.runnersworld.com/health/how-to-get
     -better-sleep-as-a-runner.

13   Erin Strout, "Rest and Recovery for Runners," *Running Times*, accessed July
     22, 2017, http://www.runnersworld.com/race-training/rest-and-recovery-for
     -runners.

14   Cindy Kuzma, "10 Things Successful Runners Do Every Night before Bed,"
     Runner's World, accessed July 22, 2017, http://www.runnersworld.com
     /sleep/10-things-successful-runners-do-every-night-before-bed.

CHAPTER 26

1   Jeff Galloway, "Share the Road," *Runner's World*, January/February 2016, 40.
     Jenny Hadfield, "The Minimalist Guide to Strength Training for Runners,"

Runner's World, accessed July 22, 2017, http://www.runnersworld.com
/ask-coach-jenny/the-minimalist-guide-to-strength-training-for-runners.

3   Cindy Kuzma, "Hop on the Habit Trail," *Runner's World*, January/February
    2015, 64–72.

4   Kelly Bastone, "Start Where You Are," *Runner's World*, January/February
    2017, 66–80.

5   Ibid.

6   Alicia Shay, e-mail to author, January 6, 2014.

7   Ibid.

8   Cindy Kuzma, "Stretch Your Limits," *Runner's World*, March 2017, 44–46.

9   Ibid.

10 Ted Spiker, "Jump In . . . " *Runner's World*, August 2014, 49–50.

CHAPTER 27

1   Christie Aschwanden, "The Big 7 Body Breakdowns," *Runner's World*,
    accessed July 22, 2017, http://www.runnersworld.com/health/the-big-7-body
    -breakdowns.

2   Michelle Hamilton, "How to Prevent Common Running Injuries," *Runner's
    World*, accessed July 22, 2017, http://www.runnersworld.com/injury
    -prevention-recovery/how-to-prevent-common-running-injuries.

3   Christie Aschwanden, "The Big 7 Body Breakdowns," *Runner's World*,
    accessed July 22, 2017, http://www.runnersworld.com/health/the-big-7-body
    -breakdowns.

4   Beth Dreher, "Get Better, Stay Better," *Runner's World*, November 2015, 60–61.

5   Amby Burfoot, "The 10 Laws of Injury Prevention," *Runner's World*, accessed
    July 22, 2017, http://www.runnersworld.com/health/the-10-laws-of-injury
    -prevention.

6   Jayme Moye, "10 Signs That You Need a Rest Day," *Runner's World*, accessed
    July 22, 2017, http://www.runnersworld.com/running-tips/10-signs-that-you
    -need-a-rest-day.

7   Ibid.

8   Alex Hutchinson, "Data Override," *Runner's World*, January/February 2016, 42.

9   Jenny Hadfield, "High Heels and Running: The Good, the Bad, and the Ugly,"
    Runner's World, accessed July 22, 2017, http://www.runnersworld.com/ask
    -coach-jenny/high-heels-and-running-the-good-the-bad-and-the-ugly.

10 Ibid.

11 "The Most Common Running and Walking Injuries," *Runner's World*,
    accessed July 22, 2017, http://www.runnersworld.com/start-running/the
    -most-common-walking-and-running-injuries.

12 Jenny McCoy, "11 Things Your Podiatrist Really Wishes You Wouldn't Do,"
    Runner's World, accessed July 22, 2017, http://www.runnersworld.com
    /feet/11-things-your-podiatrist-really-wishes-you-wouldnt-do.

13 Caitlin Carlson, "5 Tips to Help You Sidestep Injuries," *Runner's World*,
    accessed July 22, 2017, http://www.runnersworld.com/injury-prevention
    -recovery/5-tips-to-help-you-sidestep-injuries.

14 "Ask the Experts," *Runner's World*, August 2016, 52.

15 Jennifer Van Allen, "Insider Training," *Runner's World*, February 2014, 40–41.

16 A. C. Shilton, "Drug Bust," *Runner's World*, March 2015, 54–55.

17 Jessica Migala, "Fast Fixes," *Runner's World*, January/February 2017, 60.

18 Cindy Kuzma, "The Future's So Bright," *Runner's World*, March 2016, 32–33.

CHAPTER 28

1   Marc Bloom, "Should You Run When You're Sick?" *Runner's World*, accessed July 22, 2017, http://www.runnersworld.com/health/should-you-run-when-youre-sick.
2   Alex Hutchinson, "Immunity Investing," *Runner's World*, October 2016, 36.
3   Jenny McCoy, "5 Tips to Beat High Altitude Sickness," *Runner's World*, accessed July 22, 2017, http://www.runnersworld.com/illness/5-tips-to-beat-high-altitude-sickness.
4   "About Flagstaff," FlagstaffArizona.org, accessed July 22, 2017, http://www.flagstaffarizona.org/about-flagstaff.
5   "High Altitude Tips," VisitMammoth.com, accessed July 22, 2017, http://www.visitmammoth.com/high-altitude-tips.
6   Alex Hutchinson, "Blood Clots in Runners," *Runner's World*, accessed July 22, 2017, http://www.runnersworld.com/sweat-science/blood-clots-in-runners.

CHAPTER 29

1   Teal Burrell, "What Runners Should Know about Trying to Conceive," *Runner's World*, accessed July 22, 2017, http://www.runnersworld.com/pregnant-running/what-runners-should-know-about-trying-to-conceive.
2   Teal Burrell, "What You Need to Know about Running and Pregnancy," *Runner's World*, accessed July 22, 2017, http://www.runnersworld.com/pregnant-running/what-you-need-to-know-about-running-and-pregnancy.
3   Ibid.
4   Cindy Kuzma, "The Future's So Bright," *Runner's World*, March 2016, 32–33.
5   Teal Burrell, "What You Need to Know about Running and Pregnancy," *Runner's World*, accessed July 22, 2017, http://www.runnersworld.com/pregnant-running/what-you-need-to-know-about-running-and-pregnancy.
6   Pamela Nisevich Bede, "Part 2: Returning to Running after Pregnancy," *Runner's World*, accessed July 22, 2017, http://www.runnersworld.com/run-matters/part-2-returning-to-running-after-pregnancy.
7   Ibid.
8   Ibid.
9   Cindy Kuzma, "The Future's So Bright," *Runner's World*, March 2016, 32–33.
10 Teal Burrell, "What You Need to Know about Running and Pregnancy," *Runner's World*, accessed July 22, 2017, http://www.runnersworld.com/pregnant-running/what-you-need-to-know-about-running-and-pregnancy.

SECTION 6

1   Jeff Galloway, "Talk the Talk," *Runner's World*, July 2014, 30.
2   Lisa Marshall, "How to Craft a Race Plan," *Runner's World*, accessed July 23, 2017, http://www.runnersworld.com/race-training/how-to-craft-a-race-plan.
3   Emily Abbate, "Up to Speed," *Runner's World,* April 2015, 38.
4   Yishane Lee, "The Pack Rules: Don't Be Annoying," *Runner's World*, accessed July 23, 2017, http://www.runnersworld.com/race-training/running-and-racing-tips.
5   M. Nicole Nazzarro, "How to Avoid Being 'That Guy' at Your Next Race," *Runner's World*, accessed July 23, 2017, http://www.runnersworld.com/races/how-to-avoid-being-that-guy-at-your-next-race.

CHAPTER 30

1   Adam Buckley Cohen, "Ready, Set . . . " *Runner's World*, November 2014, 36.
2   Amanda MacMillan, "Is It Ever Okay to Race with Someone Else's Bib Number?" *Runner's World*, accessed July 23, 2017, http://www.runnersworld .com/racing/is-it-ever-okay-to-race-with-someone-elses-bib-number.
3   Ibid.
4   Jeff Galloway, "Deals, Pro Tips, Free Food!" *Runner's World*, October 2016, 34.
5   Lisa Marshall, "Mass Appeal," *Runner's World*, accessed July 23, 2017, http://www.runnersworld.com/race-training/why-race-with-a-pace-group.
6   "Ask the Experts," *Runner's World*, June 2015, 46.
7   Susan Paul, "What You Need to Pack in Your Gear Check Bag," *Runner's World*, accessed July 23, 2017, http://www.runnersworld.com/for-beginners -only/what-you-need-to-pack-in-your-gear-check-bag.
8   Ibid.
9   Scott Douglas, "Why You Shouldn't Freak Out about Bad Prerace Sleep," *Runner's World*, accessed July 23, 2017, http://www.runnersworld.com /newswire/why-you-shouldnt-freak-out-about-bad-pre-race-sleep.

CHAPTER 31

1   Jennifer Van Allen, "Tips for Your First Race," *Runner's World*, accessed July 23, 2017, http://www.runnersworld.com/run-nonstop/tips-for-your -first-race.
2   Cindy Kuzma, "5 Ways for Women to Discreetly Pee in Public," *Runner's World*, accessed July 23, 2017, http://www.runnersworld.com/running-tips /5-ways-for-women-to-discreetly-pee-in-public.
3   K. Aleisha Fetters, "How to Avoid Pooping during a Race," *Runner's World*, accessed July 23, 2017, http://www.runnersworld.com/health/how-to-avoid -pooping-during-a-race.
4   Ibid.
5   Dimity McDowell, "The Right Way to Carbo-Load before a Race," *Runner's World*, accessed July 23, 2017, http://www.runnersworld.com/nutrition/the -right-way-to-carbo-load-before-a-race.
6   K. Aleisha Fetters, "How to Avoid Pooping during a Race," *Runner's World*, accessed July 23, 2017, http://www.runnersworld.com/health/how-to-avoid -pooping-during-a-race.
7   Ibid.
8   Ibid.
9   Ibid.
10 Emily Abbate, "Up to Speed," *Runner's World*, April 2015, 38.

CHAPTER 32

1   Caitlin Carlson, "Oops! I Did It Again," *Runner's World*, January/February 2015, 36.
2   Susan Paul, "How to Avoid Going Out Too Fast in Your Race," *Runner's World*, accessed July 23, 2017, http://www.runnersworld.com/for-beginners-only /how-to-avoid-going-out-too-fast-in-your-race.
3   Peter Gambaccini, "A Brief Chat with Scott Douglas: Part 2," *Runner's World*, accessed July 23, 2017, http://www.runnersworld.com/newswire/a-brief-chat -with-scott-douglas-part-2.

4   Jeff Dengate, "Gear Tip: How to Get Accurate GPS Mile Pace," *Runner's World*, accessed July 23, 2017, http://www.runnersworld.com/gear-tip/gear-tip-how-to-get-accurate-gps-mile-pace.

5   Lisa Marshall, "Mass Appeal," *Runner's World*, accessed July 23, 2017, http://www.runnersworld.com/race-training/why-race-with-a-pace-group.

6   Alex Hutchinson, "Does Drafting Help in Running?" *Runner's World*, accessed July 23, 2017, http://www.runnersworld.com/sweat-science/does-drafting-help-in-running.

7   Lisa Marshall, "Race Naked," *Runner's World*, October 2015, 42.

8   Lisa Marshall, "Ace Your Race," *Runner's World*, November 2013, 83–89.

9   Brad Stulberg, "Mental Chillness," *Runner's World*, April 2017, 46–47.

10 Brad Stulberg and Steve Magness, "The 7 Habits of Highly Effective Marathoners," *Runner's World*, July 2017, 62–66.

11 Jeff Dengate, "Gear Tip: Race Day Edition," *Runner's World*, accessed July 23, 2017, http://www.runnersworld.com/gear-tip/gear-tip-race-day-edition.

12 Gail Rodgers, "Running's Greatest Bloopers," *Running Times*, accessed July 23, 2017, http://www.runnersworld.com/races/runnings-greatest-bloopers.

13 Selene Yeager, "Race-Day Disasters!" *Runner's World*, October 2012, 63–68.

14 "How to Run a Race in the Heat," *Runner's World*, accessed July 23, 2017, http://www.runnersworld.com/hot-weather-running/how-to-race-in-the-heat.

15 Alex Hutchinson, "Why Can't I Run Faster?" *Runner's World*, January/February 2016, 83–87.

CHAPTER 33

1   Dr. Jeff Brown (with Liz Neporent), "The Racer's Brain," *Runner's World*, November 2015, 83–87.

2   Sandra Gittlen, "More or Less," *Runner's World*, May 2015, 48.

3   Ibid.

4   Kelly Bastone, "This Is Not a Race," *Runner's World*, July 2015, 36–37.

5   The *Runner's World* Editors, "The Finish Pine: Awesomely Decorated Trees," *Runner's World*, accessed July 23, 2017, http://www.runnersworld.com/fun/the-finish-pine-decorated-trees.

6   "23 Cool Race Bib Collections," *Runner's World*, accessed July 23, 2017, http://www.runnersworld.com/fun/best-bib-displays.

CHAPTER 34

1   Cindy Kuzma, "You Can Fly!" *Runner's World*, June 2017, 18–20.

2   Lisa Haney, "Important Advice for Anyone Running a Big-City Race," *Runner's World*, accessed July 23, 2017, http://www.runnersworld.com/racing/important-advice-for-anyone-running-a-big-city-race.

3   Cindy Kuzma, "The Extreme Boston Marathon Ritual That Shows I've Completely Lost It," *Runner's World*, accessed July 23, 2017, http://www.runnersworld.com/other-voices/the-extreme-boston-marathon-ritual-that-shows-ive-completely-lost-it.

4   Meghan Kita, "How to Set a Guinness World Record for Racing in Costume," *Runner's World*, accessed July 23, 2017, http://www.runnersworld.com/fun/how-to-set-a-guinness-world-record-for-racing-in-costume.

5   Selene Yeager, e-mail to author, May 26, 2017.

6   Dimity McDowell, "Tips for Your Best Triathlon," *Runner's World*, accessed July 23, 2017, http://www.runnersworld.com/triathlon/tips-for-your-best-triathlon.

INDEX

Underscored page references indicate sidebars and tables.
Boldface references indicate illustrations.

Dog(s)
    running with, 137–39
    safety around, 10–11
Downhill running, <u>38</u>, 53
Drinks. *See also* Alcohol; Hydration;
    Sports drinks
    downing quickly, <u>214</u>
    types to avoid, 72, 73
    weight gain from, 85, 87
Drugs, 180, 181, 206
Dry shampoo, <u>111</u>
DVT, 187

E

Easy miles, 1
Eating
    everyday, 69–77
    for fueling runs, 57–68
    golden rules of, 55–56
    kitchen tips for, 78–81
    for long races, 210, 223
    for long runs, 33, 55–56
    before morning run, 17
    postinjury, 181
    for postrun recovery, 159
    for preventing
        gastrointestinal distress, 205–6
        side stitch, 209
    for weight loss and maintenance,
        82–91
800 meters, 25–26
Endorphins, 133
Energy bars, 86
Energy drinks, 72
Etiquette, race-day, 194–95
Evening run, motivation for,
    127–28
Expos, 199–201
Eye makeup, 111

F

Fartlek workouts, 24–25, 29–30
Faster running, training for
    cooldowns, 31–32
    Fartlek workouts, 24–25

high-intensity interval workouts,
    28–29
interval workouts, 25–26
    outdoors, 27
really hard running, 29–30
recovery during hard workouts,
    27–28
speedwork on a track, 26–27
tempo runs, 30–31
Fasting, 84
Fatigue
    during long runs, 33
    from meat-free diet, 76
    mental, 127, 128
    muscular, 21–22, 31, 36, 74, 155,
        161
    from old shoes, 94
    from overtraining, 177
Fats
    healthy, 75, 76, 84
    partially hydrogenated, 72
    in snacks, 59, 60
Feet, arch height of, 99–100, **100**
Fever, 185
Fiber, for weight loss, 89
Fig bar cookies, as midrun fuel, 61
Finish-line proposals, <u>195</u>
Fish, 74
5K races
    predictor workout for, 46
    tips for, 221–22
    warmup for, 193, 208, 221
Flat shoes, injury from, 178–79
Flat terrain, training on, 11
Flip-flops, injury from, 179
Foam rolling, 112, 159–60, <u>160</u>, 176,
    177, 181
Food. *See also* Eating; Snacks
    types to avoid, 71–73
    types to throw away, 81
Foot pain, lacing shoes to cure, 97–99,
    97, **98**, **99**
Foundation (facial), 111
400 meters, 25, 26, <u>26</u>
Fracture, stress, 174, 177
Frequency of running, 3–4
Friend, running with. *See* Running
    buddy
Fruits, 63

ABOUT THE AUTHOR

MEGHAN KITA is a writer, editor, and runner who lives in Pennsylvania's Lehigh Valley with her husband and cat. She spent six years at *Runner's World* editing and writing stories about training and racing for print and online. She's only kept count of the number of marathons she's run (17, in 10 different states), and she used to hold the Guinness World Record for fastest marathon dressed as a fast-food item (female).